AF255229

Locked In and Locked Out

Locked In and Locked Out

Tweets and Stories On Prison and
The Effects of Confinement

TONY D. VICK
JEFF NOLAND

Foreword by Jeannie Alexander

RESOURCE *Publications* · Eugene, Oregon

LOCKED IN AND LOCKED OUT
Tweets and Stories On Prison and The Effects of Confinement

Resource Publications
An Imprint of Wipf and Stock Publishers
199 W. 8th Ave., Suite 3
Eugene, OR 97401

www.wipfandstock.com

PAPERBACK ISBN: 978-1-6667-6605-9
HARDCOVER ISBN: 978-1-6667-6606-6
EBOOK ISBN: 978-1-6667-6607-3

02/15/23

DEDICATION

We who have been incarcerated have left a multitude of victims behind with lingering scars and emotional damage that we cannot undo. We pray that the prison reform we seek will help produce rehabilitation and ability for incarcerated souls to be able to effectively reintegrate back into a community without perpetuating any additional harm.

To the men and women who are trapped in captivity enduring the punishment of a retributive system, and to the men and women released from captivity who bear the scars from the lashes of inhumanity left on their souls during the years of isolation, we say: Hang On!

When you fall into the pit of prison you will never be able to escape, even when freed. But you can learn to exist in the various levels of hell created for those labeled as *felons*.

CONTENTS

PART ONE | WITHIN THE BUSINESS OF PRISON
Tony Vick

CONTENTS

PART TWO | THE AFTERMATH OF PRISON BUSINESS
Jeff Noland

FOREWORD

As I sit at my computer writing in the early summer of 2022, I am keenly aware of several things. The first is that I am writing this foreword for a dear friend for whom this will likely be his last book. Secondly, I am acutely aware that all of the hope for prison reform that so many of us, certainly including Tony Vick, have worked and fought for in the horridly retributive state of Tennessee, is being crushed right at the moment that change was within reach. I am further aware that the vanishing chance for prison and sentencing reform in Tennessee, and indeed the United States, is another foreseeable consequence of a society reaching the terminal stage of the diseases of racism and classism. I will come back to this point, as a book of this sort can only be understood, truly, in the context of the times in which it was written. What I can say with confidence is that we have learned that the center does not hold. And for those who have not yet reached that conclusion, you will.

Where then do we find hope? It is this question that brings us to the reason why a book like this matters, we find hope in the shelter of each other.

Neither of the authors of this book shield the reader from the harsh visceral reality of prison; one can smell the stench of human waste as Tony describes the hell of a days-long lockdown during the middle of summer with no air conditioning and little ventilation. The pages are unrepentantly awash with blood while in no way sensationalizing the prison experience in the manner of prison porn television, but in the most human and honest terms. As the testimony of two living witnesses, this book at its core is a theological reflection that leads the reader to a point of understanding the deep need for a restorative justice system, while neither negating the deep harm and trauma humans inflict upon each other or romanticizing the figure of the prisoner. All one is required to do is not look away. And how could we? Flannery O'Connor wrote "When you can assume that your audience holds the same beliefs you do, you can relax and use more normal means of talking to it; when you have to assume that it does not, then you have to make your vision apparent by shock—to the hard of hearing you shout, and for the almost blind you draw large and startling figures." Prison without any embellishment shouts at us and draws large and startling figures.

But that is not all that prison does. Good theology is made up not just of prophets bellowing at us from the wilderness, but also of fragile communities with broken hearts believing their God will not forsake them despite all tortuous indications to the contrary, and in that there is hope. When Tony tells us that God has never abandoned him, I think it is important to take him seriously and dig into the deeper layered meaning of that statement. For we know that it is not the knee jerk, saccharin, "God's got this," unreflective assertion of someone truly trying to avoid the weight of a terrible situation; rather, it is the whispered profession of faith in the darkness in fear and trembling hoping beyond reason for liberation—but if not, God is still God. In prison God is a God of the borderlands, in the shadows and darkness. Here one learns to apprehend God through the presence of another.

During the five years I served as a prison chaplain and Tony worked alongside me as a chaplain's clerk, my own theology turned inward toward via negativa; "Not this, not this, God is not this. God surely is not present in the concertina wire looped around the top of a twenty-foot fence. God surely is not present in this electric chair. God surely is not a goddamned system that breaks people down and destroys them for the sake of pain." And yet God is most profoundly present in the borderlands of prison, and war. In Christian theology we are taught that God is present at the moment of execution, even if we cannot feel God. Even if the Son of Man cannot feel God. God is confined to no alter nor baptismal space, no chapel, and no symbol worn around the neck. In the hard places God becomes the shared breaths in the fetid air of a locked down prison cell on a hot summer day. God is the brief stolen glance of compassion and love shared through the window of a locked door. God is the tourniquet held tight on a bleeding suicide wound. God is found in the shared meal of ramen, fake cheese, and summer smoked sausage gathered and shared—each giving what small contribution they have to make a whole. In prison one must steal their humanity back through simple insurrections of love and community.

The insurrection of love and community are most essential when the center does not hold. In many ways, the disintegration of democracy and the rise of fascism in America has been made possible by the normalization of, and our numbness to, prison.

The system of retribution, trauma, scarcity, and pain that is the American prison system, is not the logical conclusion of locking up "monsters" or "super predators," rather it is designed to continue a system of enslavement that never ended, only transformed. The product produced is not agricultural, it is human flesh and human labor. The reinvention of the plantation system relies as it always has upon the othering and objectification of the peoples and communities trapped within that system. And it is a complete objectification and dehumanization of both guard and prisoner. This is why the rate of prison staff attrition is commonly over fifty percent. You simply can't pay most people enough to sacrifice their humanity. The first step of course in ending this is amending the US Constitution and finishing the job of the Thirteenth Amendment which currently as written does not accomplish the goal of the abolition of slavery, rather it simply carved out an exception to allow enslavement of those duly convicted of a crime. And as we have seen, the exception has swallowed entire communities. In my own home of Nashville, the North Nashville zip code 37208 has the highest rate of incarceration in the country. Over 400,000 Tennessee residents have been disenfranchised by felony voter laws; not a surprise when you consider that proportionally speaking Tennessee has the tenth highest rate of incarceration in the world. We are running out of time.

The questions were asked and answered while most of us slept. What would happen if we locked up a million people? What would happen if we locked up two million people? What would happen if we disenfranchised over six million citizens because they were convicted of a felony? What would happen if we built a wall on the border? What would happen if we separated immigrant families looking for a better life, and put two-year-olds in cages and sent them to court unaccompanied by a guardian? What would happen if states passed legislation dehumanizing and challenging the personhood of queer and trans folks? What would happen if the US Capitol was subject to an attempted violent overthrow of the US government by thousands of people fueled by a transparent lie? What if the Supreme Court overturned a right to privacy and the dominos of personal rights began to fall? What if Christian Nationalist, and Fascist Christians became the political and theological identification of millions? What if is now—ushered in by decades of numbness to a growing militarized police state and carceral enslavement. We are all locked in and locked out.

And so we return to why this book matters. It is in the shelter of each other that we will find hope. It is through the common insurrections of community, comradeship, love and the willingness to bleed together, to catch each other, to make a feast out of what we can scavenge, and to have the courage to hold faith when it's all going to shit. Prison has breached the walls. At times we will have to shout and create large startling figures, and at times we must be sure to only whisper in the darkness. I am grateful for the witness of those who authored this book. Let us survive in the shelter of each other.

Jeannie Alexander
Earthfire Abbey, June 2022

TWEET:
To change how we view those in prison we must
first take a look at ourselves and decide if we
are worthy of love and forgiveness. If we are,
then everyone is. It's then that the Golden Rule
makes sense.

ACKNOWLEDGMENTS

To my dear friend, brother and co-author Jeff, thank you for being my chosen family. We have laughed, cried and struggled together through captivity and beyond, and my life has been enriched with your counsel, love and loyalty. To dear Jeannie, who showed me what was possible and dared to dream that we could make it come true, you are a beloved warrior that has loved me so unconditionally, that I have seen God in your very touch. To my fellow brothers in captivity who have been my community, my family, your stories are my stories and I pray the world will see and hear them. To sweet Tracey, who has put my words out to the world and has been a constant friend whose heart has opened to embrace a struggling soul, I owe you my gratitude. To so many others who have prayed, visited, taught, wrote, and encouraged like Janet, Richard, Lindsey, Amy-Jill, Arlene, Sam, Bruce, Julie, Rachel, Elayne, David, Bruce, Drac, Kay, and Alaina, I have been sustained and loved through you. Gratitude to Lonnie Vann, who spent hours proof-reading the manuscript. To my friends currently living in captivity, Jerry, Terrance, Alejandro, Andrew, Tavaria, Thomas, Frenchie, Howard, and so many others, I say, "Just Hang On." To the dear folks at WIPF and Stock, who took a chance on a prisoner writing a book, my heart was renewed. To my son Jonathon, I pray that I can leave a better legacy than the one I began, knowing that nothing will ever erase the pain and sorrow I caused you and so many.

Tony

ACKNOWLEDGMENTS

I would have never thought in a thousand years I would be a part of a book that I believe will be so valuable to so many who are incarcerated and those who have been released, having said that thank you Tony Vick my dear friend for taking me on this journey. I would like to thank my mother Betty and step father Murray for their never-ending encouragement while I was locked up and continuing today. I truly have the best mother ever. My two brothers Scott, Blake and entire family for not abandoning me when I needed them most. Thank you so much Scott and Sara for being there after my release, I was a wreck and would haven't made it without you. A special thanks to Dr. Chris Topley who always accepted my phone calls who stayed by my side while I was in prison. Chris literally mentored me when I started my prison sentence and then met me at the gate when I was released ten years later. I would like to thank my mother's incredible friends for the many timely letters, it seems like just when I needed to hear from the outside, your "loved and forgiven letters" arrived, so thank you Joyce, Bob, Nancy and Grace. Ginger and Jason thank you for being there after my release with love, forgiveness and lots of great food. I had my first Freedomsville Thanksgiving at your beautiful home where you actually opened your home up to me when no one else would. A huge thank you to Rev. Jeannie Alexander. If it wasn't for her guidance and support my first year out would have been a disaster. Knowing and witnessing her passion for being a prison abolitionist has helped form my goals for the rest of my days on this earth. Organizations and people like Matt Worley with Project Connect, Jenna Martin with Project Return and many other people with those organizations opened their doors and invited me in, especially when I was feeling unloved and unwanted by society. I am especially grateful for Jodi Nunes who welcomed me into a safe, compassionate, and positive work environment where people with past mistakes are accepted for who they are now.

Jeff

INTRODUCTION

These chapters may seem disconnected, weird or even bizarre. They resemble my life that is all of those things. I live in a concrete box where society has kept me now for more than a quarter of a century. Occasionally, I'm allowed to go out to play or go to do some menial chores they call work. This is prison, and it sucks.

This book has little to do with me or my sentence. Let's just go ahead and say that I deserve to be here. My crimes were horrendous and caused great harm to many people. Beyond that realization is the idea of prison itself and what that means for the moral compass of our society. I have found through my years that most people who have never been to a prison are horrified by what they see or experience when they do come inside.

It seems like a simple enough question we must ask ourselves: Are human souls worth redeeming and deserving of forgiveness? If it is a yes, then what happens inside a prison while a person is there makes a big difference to his daily existence and perhaps his successful reintegration back into society. If the answer is no, then who cares? Whatever happens, happens.

One thing is for sure, if you don't know anyone in prison at this moment, that will probably change. The likelihood of you, your family, or someone you care about going to prison is significant in the United States. The United States has the highest incarceration rate in the world. About twenty-five percent of the world's total prison population is in the United States. With these staggering numbers come a ridiculously large budget. State prisons spend as high as $69,355 per inmate (the average yearly cost of an inmate in New York). This is your tax dollars at work.

INTRODUCTION

In 2018, when Cascade released my first book, *Secrets From A Prison Cell (A Convict's Eyewitness Accounts of the Dehumanizing Drama of Life Behind Bars)* my friend, Tracy Hudson Countz, a social media professional, opened a Twitter account to promote the book. Each week I send Tweets to her and she posts them each day. Since that time the site has gained thousands of followers and has a committed audience of people involved in the prison reform movement, former incarcerated people, and loved ones of those affected by prison. The social media craze is all new to me, since none of that existed when I was free. The Twitter format of 280 characters per message, allows the reader to digest tidbits of information that may be harder to take in if presented in a different manner. I was certainly skeptical that such few characters could make any real impact on the prison reform agenda, but it has created an audience that is ready to support, email, call, or do whatever it takes to lead a conversation about change.

The best way for me to paint a picture of incarceration is to tell you about the people around me and what I'm seeing each day. But there is more to the story when it comes to incarceration. What happens after you are released? I will probably never experience that, but my best friend Jeff Noland has and is experiencing the difficult task of reintegration after being incarcerated for ten years. The second part of this book will deal with his journey and the difficulties facing those that have a prison number.

At the end of this book you'll find a practical resource guide. It's short and to the point. Why? Because you need to find a few helpful tools and stick with them, consistently and thoroughly. My hope is to give you a glimpse of incarceration and the effects of incarceration, in small enough doses to digest. There are plenty of books to give you statistical data about prisons, but those numbers are of little help to the family and friends waiting at home while their loved one is locked up. Perhaps you can use this book to help you find words to the emotions and situations you or those you love are experiencing. For the millions of us who are currently locked in to a system of injustice along with the millions who have been released from captivity who are locked out from any type of real freedom, we say: Hang On!

> **TWEET:**
> Have you ever wondered, "How in the hell did I get to this place in my life?" It's a question that haunts me sometimes. I have to redirect this question to remain sane—the new question is, "How am I going to go forward, doing better, loving better, and forgiving myself?"

AUTHOR INFORMATION

 Tony Vick has served over a quarter of a century on a life with parole sentence in Tennessee. He was born in 1962 in Clarksville, Tennessee, into a home of Southern Baptist parents and an older brother, all of which have died since his incarceration. Tony lived his life before prison as a closeted gay man, the secrets and lies led to his crimes. While in prison, Tony has worked as a tutor, newspaper editor, and clerk. He has begun book clubs, writing workshops and seminars, inmate led elder care programs, and writes about the experience of captivity in hopes to add context to the current prison reform movement. In 2018, his essays and poems, *Secrets from A Prison Cell: A Convict's Eyewitness Accounts of the Dehumanizing Drama of Life Behind Bars*, was published by Cascade Books, 2018. His works have been included in multiple books and publications, most recently *Pensive: A Global Journal of Spirituality and the Arts*; *A 21st Century Plague: Poetry from a Pandemic*, by Elayne Clift; *The Avocet: A Journal of Nature Poetry*; *Turning Teaching Inside Out* by Davis and Roswell; *Keep Watch with Me: An Advent Reader for Peacemakers*; *Abandoned Mine*; *Storms of the Inland Sea: Poems of Alzheimer's and Dementia Caregiving*. He furnishes *Tweets* for @cellsecrets.

AUTHOR INFORMATION

Jeff Noland served ten years in a Tennessee prison and was released in 2020. He was born in 1964 in Dallas, Texas, into a two-parent home, whose parents were Baylor University graduates. His parents divorced when he was ten and both remarried. Jeff has three brothers, one died from an auto accident at age fourteen. Jeff has played music all of his life and is the reason he moved from Texas to Tennessee, where he worked in retail management. While incarcerated, Jeff took courses from Union University, facilitated Celebrate Recovery, played music in the church, organized community activities and successfully completed TRICOR job placement programing. Since his release from prison, Jeff found a house and a job he loves, organized a legal/support group for people on the registry, volunteers at No Exceptions Prison Collective, and is part of several community activities for disenfranchised people. Along with music, he loves to run, play tennis, and kayak. Contact Jeff at jeffnoland64@gmail.com.

Foreword author: Rev. Jeannie Alexander is the executive director of No Exceptions Prison Collective (https://www.orgnoexceptionsprisoncollective.org). She is also a co-founding resident of Harriet Tubman House, an interfaith community dedicated to restorative practices in earth stewardship and human rights. She has been a professor of Philosophy, Ethics, and Religion. She is a writer with essays published in several books, including *And The Criminals With Him (Essays in Honor of Will D. Campbell and All the Reconciled)* by Cascade Books, 2012. She is interviewed, lectures, and preaches frequently on the topics of mass incarceration as slavery, alternatives to prison, and transformative justice. She holds a JD from Cornell Law and a Masters in Religious Studies.

PART ONE

Within The Business Of Prison

TONY VICK

TWEET:
There are more like us all over the world—
confused, who can't remember the name of
their dog or the smell of sweet blossoms—
gazing from barred windows into a field of
concrete and razor wire. We pray that all our
memories will not fade.

TWEET:

Imagine:

That one day all humans incarcerated will find ways to reconciliation. That tortures of prison will be replaced with avenues for redemption. Just as insiders need forgiveness, the world's citizens need forgiveness for the treatment of souls behind bars.

"The unexamined life is not worth living"

—Socrates, Plato's Apology

MIRROR, MIRROR

The first week I was in prison I walked over to the steel sink-toilet combo that was near my cell door. It was a cold room, void of any color or life. The mirror was a flat polished piece of steel that reflected a circus image of my face.

I stared at the fuzzy image in front of me and wondered if I could face all the demons I had buried so deep in my soul. If I opened up the deep wounds that had been stuffed with the gauze of self-hatred and unworthiness, I didn't know if I could ever make it in my new world of violence and chaos.

All the false pretenses, lies, manipulation and avoidance of reality seemed ridiculous at this point. It was too much. I looked intently into that steel mirror and told myself that I had to face the truth. I was determined that whatever type of life I was about to have in this God-awful place, was going to be based on truth and authenticity—even if it killed me. The façade of a straight, Christian, successful family man was transformed into the gay, broken, failure of a man that was actually standing there.

I was a murderer. Guilt from the destruction, devastation and disappointment I caused pressed against me like a sweaty t-shirt.

People had told me about the healing power of forgiveness, but I couldn't imagine anyone forgiving me, certainly I didn't feel I was worthy of forgiveness.

I knelt on that dusty concrete floor and prayed to a God I've always believed in and was terrified of. My heart burst open like a broken dam and I wept and sobbed until another tear could not flow. The fracturing of my soul allowed God's love to creep in and a strange comfort held my heart like a precious baby. I knew that somehow things would be okay.

Even though I realized the hurt that I caused so many may be too deep for them to ever find forgiveness for me, I knew that I had to forgive and let go of the anger that brought me here. I forgave my parents who created a fear in my heart that being gay was a curse of God and could never be forgiven. I forgave the church who told me that homosexuals would burst hell wide open, I forgave all the bullies from school who called me names and destroyed my self-worth. I let it all go.

I had never lived an authentic life before. I was walking on new territory. Prison was going to be my home, my life, my existence forever. Whatever good I wanted to accomplish, however I wanted to shape my legacy must be done in captivity, behind the razor wire that separates me from the world.

> **TWEET:**
> If you should enter these prison gates one day do not abandon all hope. Instead, know that each day you are alive, there is always another chance, there is always that mysterious expectation. There is always hope. Fight for it, every day!

GLIMPSES OF SELF-HATE FROM PRISON

People of earth,

Do you think I care about what you think about me? Apparently I do. I've lied, cheated, and killed because I cared so much. You liking me was my top priority. Having your love was my main concern. You didn't love me, you loved the perception of me because I was hidden beneath layers of protection. The protection of my deep secrets. If you knew them your love would stop. And love was a drug that I was addicted to. I would do whatever it took to get my drug. Anything.

I can't allow events to occur organically. I must manipulate, orchestrate, maneuver, or organize the situation. I need control. Lack of control makes me vulnerable and scared. My control has changed my destiny. If I had reacted to life, instead of manipulating life—would my life be better? I should have trusted the universe, the God of life to move me through his maze. Instead, I jumped over the puzzle's walls to take a different path. It seems the path I chose is through the dark, wooded forest with monsters and earthquakes.

Depression hits me like a wave pounding the hard rocks on the cliff. It floods my heart and mind with emotions that I can't control. It drowns my hopes and dreams, and all the joy from my being. It flows through my veins like a burning hot lava. Let it end, let it stop. My heart feels cracked and devoured of life blood. Why does my fear keep me from ending it? I can stop the pain if only my courage allowed. But I stop myself, even more depressed because I am such a coward. How did my conscience fail me? I detest acts of violence, prejudice, and egotists. Yet my own arrogance prevented me from exposing my true nature. It allowed me to deceive, destroy, and corrupt the lives of others. What a hypocrite!

Dad I love you. Dad I hate you. You were always supportive. You were so prejudiced. You were kind to everyone—as long as they were not homos. "Accept Jesus—go to heaven" you preached. "Except the gays who are blasphemous." Murderers and thieves can be forgiven, but abominations of homosexuality cannot. Where does your love come from? Where does your hate come from?

> **TWEET:**
> Sometimes I have to fight like a drowning
> victim for air to stop myself from falling into
> the pit of depression. History has taught me to
> fight—once you've landed at the bottom of the
> pit, climbing your way out is nearly impossible.
> Grab those scattered roots to stop your fall.

ALL IS WELL

I must be hard-headed, stubborn or just plain crazy. That is what I imagine God must think of my actions occasionally, or perhaps more often than not. Amazingly, he keeps on finding ways to encourage and love me in the most profound and special ways. For me, the trouble comes when I keep my blinders on when trying to get through the mundane tasks of the day and fail to see God's mighty hands at work all around me.

Like it or not, prison is my home, and as far as I can tell at this moment, will be until I bite the dust. So I work hard at building community and trying to form classes and workshops that benefit all of us. And selfishly, it creates a family around me and I don't feel so alone. Even then, at times these walls of my small cell seem to cave in on me, burying me under the weight of depression and isolation.

So many of my friends have died behind these walls—some quickly, others lingering for days, weeks or months, until their bodies finally gave out. I guess if one has a life sentence like I do, death should not be such a troubling occurrence. Whatever state we find ourselves in—free, incarcerated, guilty or innocent—the process of dying causes a lot of anxiety. I wonder if the souls of all those who have died behind these walls linger around waiting for freedom—or if their souls are free to dance around—no shackles or chains?

I had a medical appointment recently and was required to wait in the infirmary hallway because an out-of-control inmate was being escorted into an isolation room. The hallway has six rooms housing inmates who are in need of medical care. They are reserved for the worst of the worse—so to be there is bad. I peeked through the window of one of the rooms and saw Benny, an old buddy I hadn't seen in weeks. I tapped on the door and he eventually looked up from the bunk but seemed not to recognize me. He had a startled, unknowing expression on his face, and looked frightened and disoriented. His naked body was barely covered with a sheet and fresh wounds were all over his exposed skin. It looked as though he had scratched himself with his long, uncut nails.

I could not take my eyes off of him—I was paralyzed with wonderment and disgust. He began screaming out, "Where is Connie—where is Connie?" I knew from our many previous talks that Connie was his wife who had died a decade ago. The last time we talked Benny told me a few of the same old stories he recounted every time I had seen him the last three years. His memory was failing, but I had seen worse from old guys. He still took care of himself, even though he did not have a prison job and had not for some time. As always, I told him to holler at me if he needed anything. What transpired that had brought him to this state? Benny is still in the infirmary, and has been for weeks. The prison staff will not tell us what is going on with him, and I don't know if he has family or friends on the street that care about him.

Benny is like so many that have passed before me. I currently have friends inside the walls that are facing gradual forms of dementia, and others who have parents or loved ones who are in states of mental decline. I too fear, that my body will outlive my mind and I will be like Benny, alone in a cold isolated cell, left to die. Perhaps it is best not to know what is happening to you when you are in a condition like that.

And before I allow my mind to spiral off into the "what ifs" and the "oh my God's"—I have to remember that God has never failed me. The times that I have sinned so terribly that forgiveness seemed like an impossible notion, God's words have offered me that forgiveness. When free people can't find the place to offer redemption and reconciliation, God has reached out his hand and welcomed me home. He has taken me through every dark valley, every pain, every struggle, and every situation that has developed. The moments that I have felt unworthy, unloved and betrayed by all my friends, God has wrapped me in his arms so tightly that the distance diminished between us.

Even though I may not understand what Benny is going through, the same God that watches over me is watching over him. It pains me to watch Benny and anyone go through such physical and mental torture. I must remember, that when my own body is faced with such a burden—*All is well*.

TWEET:

When the walls of depression begin to cave in on you, is when you need your community to help hold up the structure. But in order to have a community to do so, you must work hard at building it by demonstrating compassion and empathy for others.

DOES A 51-YEAR LIFE SENTENCE MAKE SENSE FOR JUVENILES?

It took the jury only thirty minutes on that Wednesday afternoon to decide that Alejandro Gauna, who was seventeen at the time of the crime, was guilty of first degree murder. The choice before them after that, was only two-fold: A Life Sentence with the Possibility of Parole, or Life Without Parole. This decision proved not be as easy as the first—a hung jury. Therefore, the judge was left to pass sentence of Life With the Possibility of Parole. So on May 8, 2008, Tipton County Judge Joseph Walker turned young Alejandro over to the Tennessee Department of Corrections.

The sentence Alejandro received for first degree murder in Tennessee really didn't make much difference. You see, effectively Tennessee has three death sentences for murder, since *Life With the Possibility of Parole* means the person must serve fifty-one years before parole eligibility can even be considered. Fifty-one years in prison is an unrealistic time to survive incarceration. Then of course, there is the *Death Penalty* and the *Life Without Parole sentence*.

Tennessee is the only state where a life sentence with the possibility of release is fifty-one years. The national average for life with the possibility of release is twenty-five years. Actually, before the Clinton Crime Bill was enacted and Tennessee's version adopted in 1995—twenty-five years was the minimum standard in Tennessee.

Alejandro began life in Austin, Texas in what appeared to be a blessed two-parent home, attending church and excelling in school.

Living on the outskirts of violent housing projects, it was always in Alejandro's peripheral vision that danger lurked very close by, often seeing the police chasing people through his back yard. At fourteen, Alejandro's life was about to change, his parents, both Mexican-American, divorced. Alejandro's world was broken and the chaos that developed sent him into a downward spiral—from dropping out of school in the ninth grade, hanging out with the wrong crowd, running away from home to escape the dysfunction, to getting hooked on drugs and then selling drugs to survive. He found himself in and out of juvenile detention centers and rehab, until he eventually simply ran away. Like so many who find themselves running from something, what they run towards turns out just as bad or worse as the horrors they are trying to escape. Already traumatized by the craziness of addiction and bad influences did not help Alejandro's mental stability when he was robbed at gunpoint and felt very close to dying, still at fourteen years old. The only thing he knew to do to feel somewhat safe at that point was to carry a gun.

On January 1, 2007, at age seventeen, Alejandro and a friend, drove to Tennessee to sell the only asset they had to offer—marijuana. When State Trooper Calvin Jenks pulled the two over for speeding, the decisions Alejandro made in a few moments would end two people's lives: The Trooper's and Alejandro's. In a hazy and scared attempt to get away, Alejandro fired two bullets into Trooper Jenks, and life ended.

As horrific as this crime is, the fact that a seventeen-year-old committed it has to be considered. According to the Juvenile Law Center:

> "Scientific research shows key developmental differences between youth and adults that impact a youth's decision making impulse control, and susceptibility to peer pressure. While these differences do not excuse youth from responsibility for their actions, the US Supreme Court has reportedly recognized that youth are less blameworthy than adults and more capable of change and rehabilitation." (Roger vs Simmons, Graham vs Florida)

If Alejandro's attorney, Blake Ballin would have called the expert witness, Dr. James S. Walker, who was prepared to testify, the jury would have received forensic psychological evidence that may have weighed on their decision. According to Dr. Walker:

> "My evaluation of Mr. Gauna revealed that he was suffering from several mental health conditions at the time of his offense, including major depression, cannabis intoxication, formaldehyde intoxication, and antisocial/paranoid personality characteristics. His ability to act in a premeditated fashion was impaired at the time of the crime by his mental conditions." (James S. Walker, PhD, October 22, 2013, Clinical Neuropsychologist and Forensic Psychologist)

An estimated 250,000 youth are tried, sentenced, or incarcerated as adults every year across the US (http://www.njjn.org). Despite the establishment of a separate juvenile system over a century ago—youth routinely are charged and prosecuted in adult criminal justice systems. During the 1990s, the era when many of our most punitive criminal justice policies were developed—forty-nine states altered their laws to increase the number of minors being tried as adults.

According to 2017 data from Tennessee Department of Correction, there are 1,294 individuals in Tennessee prisons serving a fifty-one-year life sentence. Over half of these individuals were youthful offenders (between the ages of eighteen and twenty-five) or juveniles (below the age of eighteen) on the date of the offense. Specifically, 115 were below the age of eighteen.

Alejandro is contrite when recounting his story, first acknowledging the incredible harm he has done by taking an innocent life and all the pain he has caused the community and families. Now after being incarcerated nearly fifteen years, and enduring all the difficulties of a juvenile entering an adult system, his regrets are many, from not finishing school, starting drugs, and picking up a gun to feel safe. As he has matured, Alejandro has taken advantage of every opportunity for growth and education offered him. He earned his general equivalency diploma the very first year of incarceration, got involved with church programs, took business classes led by Stan Olson for five years, took part in speaking to youth groups visiting the prison, attended classes through Union University, received his barber's license, and now is working with Tennessee Rehabilitative Initiative in Corrections, as a graphic designer. This company operates from within the prison and helps offenders to transform themselves by providing continuous preparation and assistance through the context of work and career management. Their ultimate goal is to prepare offenders for success after release.

Many advocacy groups are working hard to change the life sentence laws in Tennessee, one in particular, No Exceptions Prison Collective, has worked six years on this very issue. Reverend Jeannie Alexander, the Co-Founder said:

> "No Exceptions has worked to educate communities and legislators concerning this inhumane and draconian fifty-one-year life sentence, and we have supported legislation that would reduce the fifty-one years back to twenty-five years for a possibility of parole for everyone with that sentence. No Exceptions does not stand alone in this fight; we stand with families across the state who are demanding that their loved ones have a real chance to return home. Accountability does not require death; it does not require an exile ending in death."

It does look like Tennessee is headed for making some important and moral decisions regarding their sentencing laws. Senator Raumesh Akbari out of Memphis, noted in a March 6, 2019 *Tennessean* article:

> "Many young defendants face childhood hardships and trauma that can be overcome with time and treatment. It's so complicated when you're dealing with loss of life, but we are talking about children. As horrific as it sounds that a child committed murder, the person they are now is not the person they will be in twenty years."

Perhaps in the near future we will begin making a transition for Tennessee laws and for Alejandro. Through the hard work of No Exceptions Prison Collective led by Reverend Alexander along with many other advocacy groups, we will eventually acknowledge that justice does not look like making people disappear forever; justice is about healing, transforming, and true accountability. Vengeance is not justice.

> **TWEET:**
> How will history reflect on our generation's ideology of keeping its citizens confined for years and years without much thought of re-integration? You believe all life has value or you don't. Pro Life means caring from the womb to the tomb and all the messy parts in between.

WHAT IF TONIGHT WAS IT?

(That is, if I was a free man. A parody of life and death worries)

When you close your eyes they will never open again. You fall into the eternal slumber of death. If you knew that, what would be on your Top Ten must do list?

For me:

1. Pray—make sure me and God are cool. I don't want any unexpected consequences.
2. Take a look around the place to ensure any odd things are thrown out—I don't want those packing my belongings to have "Oh my God" moments.
3. Leave my Will out in the open—I don't want family members fighting over money when they should be mourning their loss.
4. Leave my coffee table books about roses open to my favorite "Yellow Rose of Texas." I don't want my family picking cheapass carnations for my casket pall.
5. Delete the history of my browsers, just in case.
6. Order a delivery pizza for 11:00 p.m.—I should be sound asleep by then. That way maybe they will find my body before it gets too, you know.
7. Put my new PJ's on that Janice gave me for my birthday—too slick to wear in bed, but will be nice for body retrieval.

8. Don't eat anything heavy—I heard you take your last dump after you go, so I don't want to leave a big mess, and ruin my silk pj's.

9. Throw away my glasses. I hate seeing a corpse laying in the casket with glasses, as if you are going to need them for all eternity. I don't plan on doing any reading.

10. Put on some nice music, light a candle, ambiance is everything. Take a sleeping pill—I don't think I'll sleep otherwise. And I want to be fast asleep when I go to the "Upper Room"— it may be a bumpy ride.

TWEET:
I did not realize the gate I would step through
would be the entrance to my tomb. I should
have turned around for one more gaze at
freedom and sucked in one more breath of air
not confined.

ADAPTING

Even in the confines of prison, where I've been for twenty-six years, I usually manage to have a plan or a strategy of dealing with the day-to-day craziness that ensues. The pandemic introduced a new energy to the prison system and it brought along a fear that has unsettled an already jittery group. I'm living in a petri dish of shared germs and inability to disinfect, wash, or get away from other people.

I don't think that most of us who are incarcerated are in great fear of contracting the virus—that is simply inevitable. Eventually a person who works here will undoubtedly bring the contagion in and it will spread like lice at a kindergarten. So we sit and wait for it to come. Those of us who have underlying health issues understand that the prison medical system already has major flaws in times of normalcy—so we can't imagine how it will deal with a radical situation.

People in the freeworld have their own worries—how to pay bills, self-isolating, buying food, getting medical attention and an array of problems that seem foreign to me at the moment. I watch and hear the stories in the media of families loosing loved ones and not being able to visit those elderly family members in nursing homes. Others who wait for hours in food bank lines or worrying about where and if they can get tested. Scary times.

Within the prison walls we are scared to present a cough or a sneeze or any other symptom that may cause the staff to isolate us. Such symptoms cause us to be placed in segregation, a place normally reserved for those who get in trouble, a place that has nothing but cold steel and concrete, the last place any of us want to go. You leave behind your articles of property, which may be lost or stolen, you may not even get back to the same cell where you have formed friendships or community, and who knows how long you will have to stay in segregation once you are placed there. So it's not surprising that inmates who may be sick are not going to the medical clinic for assistance or drawing attention to their symptoms—*fear.*

When we are lined up to get our temperatures checked, one hundred and twenty-eight inmates fall silent as we wait our fate. Each time I clear the line, I begin to breathe again and pray this will all soon be over. One thing this pandemic has reinforced in my mind is that whichever side of the prison wall we live, we all have fears and emotions that are associated with separation from each other. Humans are meant to share experiences—good and bad, and to embrace life as a community.

This will all pass eventually, but the fear of unknown enemies has been formed in our hearts—and that will not pass easily. What can be reinforced, is that we can find ways to support each other whatever the circumstances are, and we will always find a way to get through, because we are resilient pieces of art formed by God that can mold and thrive in any situation. All we need is time to adapt.

Author's note: Turns out that practically everyone did get COVID-19 in the prison where I was housed. Many went to the hospital, placed on ventilators, and some died. RIP to our brothers who escaped from the bounds of razor wire and found freedom on the other side.

TWEET:

Between COVID and short staffing the
prison has not had any church in two years.
Amazingly, those of various faiths have
come together in the unit for prayer and
encouragement. We refuse to rely on prison
administration to dictate when we can gather
for spiritual matters.

TWEET:
I get mail occasionally from folks who have
read my book about prison where they inform
me: "If you hadn't done your crime you would
not be in prison, so deal with it." I write back:
"Thank you for your letter, it was the highlight of
my day, receiving mail—so deal with it."

MAIL CALL

Every day at around six in the evening, one hundred and twenty-eight inmates, including myself, wait with great anticipation if our names will be called at mail call. Some, have stopped coming out of their cells for the event, after being disappointed day after day with no mail, but others, like myself, can't help but to linger with the continued hope that someone from outside these concrete walls is thinking about us.

The art of writing a letter has changed and mostly diminished over my decades of incarceration. Most free world people these days don't bother to buy envelopes or stamps, or shop for lovely stationary to put pen to paper—communication is sent through a few clicks on a keyboard or phone. But I have managed to retain a few pen pals through the years who still bother with such things and faithfully ensure I have some occasional mail at our callout.

Mail receiving, opening, and reading is a ritual for me that has become as special as someone coming in person to visit or getting a hug. It's a procedure involved that allows me to appreciate all the hands who have been involved in getting this hug to me. I begin with admiring the stamp chosen My pen pals never use the standard "flag" postage stamp, but choose colorful, artistic ones that scream out with purposes and causes. The vibrant colors stand out amongst the grey tones that dominate my surroundings. I carefully remove the stamp and place it in my book collection, noting the month and year of receipt.

I examine all the postal markings along with the date it was processed through the postal machine which helps me know when it was placed in the mailbox. The address and return address writing indicates if my pen pal was in a hurry or relaxed when the envelope was addressed. Is the writing clear and attractive or jumbled and scribbly?

I carefully open the envelope and smell the contents. Often I can tell what the person writing was doing before placing the letter in the envelope—cooking, chopping food, just washed hands, gardening—all whiffs of free world air and activities, which are all cleansing aromas to my senses, and allows me to be in the presence, just for a second of my friend.

Every word is read and reread many times until I have consumed the content and can respond in kind with my own letter. Over the years the letters I receive have gotten fewer and less frequent, and I miss the hugs. Fortunately, I have hidden away a few of the special pieces of mail that have meant so much to me. One in particular is from my mother, who has long since passed. Her letter has survived multiple shakedowns and moves, floods, and other stresses associated with prison life. When I am especially lonely, I hold my mother's letter and can still feel her presence and love—the swirls of her "S's" and the way she dots her "I's" (just off center)—and the way she always signed her letters to me "My precious son, mama loves you." And now, twenty years after her death, she is still sending me love and hope through that one piece of mail.

Mail, these days, the kind that puts pen to paper, are artifacts that will tell stories and send love to people for years to come. For those of us who are incarcerated, each piece of mail is like winning the lottery—the heart racing joy of hearing the guard yell out "Vick, you've got mail,"—still brings me out of my cell and waiting with hopeful anticipation each day at six o'clock in the evening.

TWEET:

I love writing letters connecting with people.
The ink bled upon the page represents where
I am, who I am, and puts me in their hands,
embraced and loved. If you would like to be
my pen pal, please let me know, I would love to
connect with you.

I CLEANED MY FLOOR TODAY

I woke up to violence and chaos this morning—inmates running around talking about fights breaking out on the compound, stabbings, and a lockdown looming very soon. People are scurrying about getting ice or a quick shower anticipating days being locked in the cell unable to get either. I wondered if the blood spatter on my pants would wash out or if I would have to throw them away. Even if I could get the blood out, the memories of metal blades being plunged into nearby bodies or the fear captured on the faces of victims would not be easily forgotten.

I gathered my old rags and made some soapy water in my plastic trashcan. Soon I was on my hands and knees scrubbing the floor, starting from the back wall, where I had to get on my belly to reach under the bunk. The cool concrete floor felt good against my skin and solid under my bones. This was a comfortable place, low to the ground, doing a mundane task in spite of the crises pending around me. This I could control.

My cellee sat silent on his bunk understanding this was my routine. I don't attempt to analyze my actions while scrubbing the floor—I just do, allowing my emotions and fear to be released through my aggressive rubbing of rag to floor, rag to floor. And there on my knees is where I find God, the Great Comforter, the Prince of Peace, and there I find rest. I remember my breath. *Breathe—breathe.* My quivering stomach settles down, all is well.

> **TWEET:**
> I'm always scared. Can you imagine spending every waking moment scared? After a while that quiver in your stomach is like an annoying friend that you can't escape. It keeps you on your toes, conscious of what is around the corner. But the stress is a killer.

THREE DAYS

(A reflection of three consecutive days in captivity)

Day One

Breathing is something we take for granted—we just do it. The alternative is death. In this small room today are eight grown men, fellow inmates, sitting on the floor talking about our breaths. Outside the door, we hear dominos slamming on the metal tables, music blaring, arguments over the sports game on TV last night, and a big collaborative chatter that blends into one big hum.

It's challenging to find our breath. We inhale intentionally breathing in the negative energy around us, then exhale a calming peace into this confining, concrete space. We find a unison breath and live in this state—for a time, at least. If we could just stay here and never leave the serenity that supplants the fear and rage within this violent razor wire cage.

We find our yoga poses, stretching muscles, always tense from constant fear of being assaulted, shanked or raped. Ironically, we end in corpse pose, trying not to admit to ourselves that we could face that reality at any time. At least, for now, we are able to rise from corpse pose. We have seen many body bags with flesh in eternal corpse pose carted out before us. We look at each other as we open the door to leave, as if to say, "Good luck, till next time."

Day Two

I spent a lot of time in my cell this day, absorbing it like never before. The emotions held by the previous inhabitants were saturating my soul. The walls in this cell are so scarred by emotional graffiti that they appear to swirl and shift, like thick, white smoke trapped in a glass case. I sense, that for many men of this cell, each day was a struggle. Alive but not living, feeling everything, feeling nothing. Some may have been tired of existing, and longing to join those who truly know peace, the dead.

I sense bodies leaning against the steel door, eyes watching for signs of life on the other side. I feel the deep breaths taken amid the isolated tension of confinement. The walls are talking to me today and I cannot help but to shed some tears for them, for me. I cannot overlook the scratched letters at the end of my bunk where the gray paint peeled off to the black metal below: "SOS." I pray his help came before it was too late. Just above me, on the plastic light cover, written in black marker, "Fuck Prison"—and each time I see it, I affirm that sentiment. I have not tried to erase it or remove it—it deserves to be there, it deserves to be seen, heard, *yelled!* In my cave dwelling, ancestors of confinement have engraved drawings to express pain, frustration, struggle—in order to recognize and to remember that they were alive and present. At least for that day.

Day Three Lockdown

5:30 a.m.: We wake up to a lockdown at the prison this morning, a bag with a bologna sandwich and a saltine cracker was our breakfast. When something violent happens or when it's a gang thing—and it is usually a gang thing, it is common for the prison to go on lockdown. No inmate is allowed outside of their cell, and more than likely, the shakedown crew will come in and turn your cell inside out looking for weapons, drugs, etc.

7 a.m.: The water is shutdown so no toilets or sink water. I guess they don't want inmates flushing contraband. If I have to pee or shit I'll have to just do it, and cover the toilet with a towel in order to avoid the stench or look of it while I'm eating a foot away from it. I do live in a small bathroom, by the way.

7:15 a.m.: I heard the unit officer say that twenty-three shanks were found in the unit beside mine, mostly in one cell. Gang leaders don't usually keep weapons or drugs in their cells—they let an underling hold them. So many found in one cell indicates that the gang was planning a major attack on another group. The last few days we have seen a lot of violence, people taken to the hospital, blood, so much blood. Luckily no staff member has been injured this week.

8 a.m.: My cellee can't hold it, he has to use the toilet. I lay on my bunk and turn my head toward the wall in order to give him some sense of privacy.

8:20 a.m.: I go ahead and add to the sludge pool with my own bodily functions. I cover the toilet with a towel, and we both pretend we are not sitting so close to an open sewer. To acknowledge the shit so close, would be recognizing that we are not human at this moment, but part of the animal kingdom in the wild that has not learned the courtesies of flushing.

9:30 a.m.: The electricity is turned off—why, I don't know. It doesn't take long for the room to heat up since the temperature outside is in the mid nineties. My cellee and I look at each other with similar expressions of dread and fear about what the rest of the day holds. We sprinkle baby powder around the room to cover the smell of the toilet gatherings now being heated by the warmth of the room.

11 a.m.: We begin to hear loud talking and doors slamming in our unit and look to see the shake down crew entering. It looks to be about twenty men and women dressed in all black, holding taser guns, pepper spray bombs and handcuffs. This is it.

11:10 a.m.: They begin on the bottom floor—I'm on top. I see two crew go and stand in front of the first ten cells, ready to enter and extract the inmates. The inmates must strip naked, lift their sack, turn, spread their butt cheeks, squat and cough. By doing so, if someone had crammed something up their ass the squatting and coughing may push it out. They inspect your asshole to see if anything looks unusual. After twenty-six years of this routine, I've mostly lost all sense of humility. The male staff do this procedure to the male inmates, the female staff wait outside the door. After looking over your naked body, the inmate is then allowed to put his boxers on, get handcuffed, and walked to a room in the unit, told to sit on the floor and face the wall. No talking, no looking up, keep your head towards the floor at all times.

1:00 p.m.: The crew finally reach my cell upstairs. Even though my cellee and I know that we don't have any weapons or drugs in the cell, the nerves hit and I can see our shallow breaths begin and the wonder of how our belongings will be destroyed in this process. We are walked to the waiting room and sit and wait for the crew to finish searching our cell.

1:35 p.m.: We are walked back to our cell, the door closes, and we look at each other wondering where to begin to put all this mess back to-gether. It looks like a tornado has hit. Papers, letters and books that were on the shelves are now scattered about the floor. His, mine, who knows what is what. The melted water left in our ice chests that we were using to drink is now poured all over the floor, saturating a lot of our paper belongings. Cherished letters, pictures and books that we bought, now wet. We try to save what we can by hanging the paper stuff about the room to dry. It's like coming back to your house after it's been burglarized. The violation you feel by strangers fingering over your stuff is hard to bear. The half-eaten bag of cookies along with my bottle of Tylenol purchased on commissary are floating in the toilet. I'll have to fish them out before the water comes back on or the toilet will get clogged and more water will be running all over the floor.

2:00 p.m.: My cellee sits down in the floor and begins to weep. His guitar has been broken, the wood has been cracked somehow during the shakedown. I feel his pain, but leave him alone in order to get himself together.

4:00 p.m.: We have saved what we can and bagged up the rest to take out to garbage when we can. I feel nasty, sweaty, and wonder when the water and electricity will be turned back on. The crew has been gone from our building for over an hour.

4:45 p.m.: They bring another brown bag with a cheese sandwich and a saltine cracker, we put them aside—the thought of eating seems ridiculous at this moment.

9:30 p.m.: The water and electricity is turned back on. We run the water for a while till it runs clear again. We take turns washing ourselves in the sink. We make up some soapy water to clean the floor and walls the best we can.

10:45 p.m.: We settle into bed in silence. All I can think is how long till the next one and try not to dread it already. I pray for sleep to come.

> **TWEET:**
> I now understand why a caged animal will
> always face the door opening. Looking toward
> the exit does provide a sense of hope—surely, one
> day it will open again, and when it does, I will run
> out and be free and loved and held. *Surely!*

A PAGE TURNER CAN BE A LIFE CHANGER

Discussing the virtues of Atticus Finch in Harper Lee's, *To Kill A Mockingbird*, or Napoleon's evil dissent in George Orwell's *Animal Farm*, takes on a new perspective when the book club is in prison with a group of inmate's leading the conversation. Paralleling the criminal justice system from the eyes of those who often feel that "justice" was not in the scenario, along with the flawed novel characters, proved to be a spirited debate. This served to be one of the main reasons I started a prison book club—thought provoking consideration of new ideas and ways of thinking.

I look around the room and I see thirteen amazing men whom I've come to call friends. In the mix are those who have murder charges, drug charges, along with everything in between. If someone only looked at the rap sheets of our book club members, they may conclude that the person described is a hopeless, ignorant criminal without any hope of redemption. However, without the banner declaring each one a *felon*, a person sitting in the room with these intelligent, compassionate and hopeful men, may reach a totally different conclusion.

Providing avenues for people to examine and consider various approaches to situations allows them to make better decisions when presented with difficult roads to choose from. Being able to read and analyze how characters in a book make decisions, many times the wrong ones, helps create those "light bulb" moments that can change the trajectory of a wrong course. It's amazing to see these grown men of the book club tear up when reflecting on a particular character and the trials and tribulations he is enduring. The relief of emotion projected in those tears are a needed escape from the walls of protection that has been built around our hearts in this hostile place.

Our book club has read some amazing books, from those mentioned above, to Simon Wisenthol's, *The Sunflower* that explores the capacity of forgiveness—that one hit home for real. We read Janet Wolf's book, *Practicing Resurrection (The Gospel of Mark and Radical Discipleship)*, where the author explores the concepts and stories found in the book of Mark, through the lens of prison. In fact, the author reached out to us with an incredible offer to come and talk with our group. It was amazing sitting around a table asking the author questions about the material she wrote and experiencing the humanity she brought to our book club.

We have men eagerly waiting for an opportunity to get involved with our club—so we are sharing books and passing them around. It's a great thing—to see a desire for community and discussion in this place. A generous benefactor has blessed us with books for our club, Arlene Katz, who has been instrumental in making it a success. I hope she understands how she is helping to change lives and build community from miles away from where she lives.

To be involved in prison ministry one doesn't always have to visit a prison in person. Many folks are pen-pals to insiders, others advocate by speaking up for prison reform in their community, and then there is simply voting for candidates that share a desired vision about where our prison system is and where it is heading. The characters in the books we read bring a sense of humanity and understanding to insiders when others are not available to do so. Words are pure gold in this place, coming from letters or from books.

The men in our book club have become a family that can trust each other and find ways to search for commonality instead of confrontation. We have allowed ourselves to cry, laugh and hear truth in a place typically not welcomed to do so. These concrete walls and razor wire are lost when we open a book and begin to explore life outside of this place. Each page provides one more moment where our minds are free from the brutality and fear that exists all around us.

To all the people who write us, love us, pray for us, visit us, and work toward prison reform: *Thank you!*

TWEET:

Our unit library we call *Books By Kay*, created by the generosity of @kaycanal, is the center of activity. Guys lined up outside of this little closet where our librarian, Lonnie Vann, checks out the books to eager readers—an example of how one person can change hundreds of lives.

There is far too much law for those who can afford it
and far too little for those who cannot.

—DEREK BOK

INNOCENT

There are a lot of "innocent" people in prison, but just saying it doesn't make it so. And it really doesn't matter if it is true or not—the bottom line is that the man standing in front of the judge at sentencing becomes whatever label the judge places on him, "Guilty" or "Not Guilty." Once inside the steel bars getting another chance to change that label is an uphill battle that is timely, costly and detrimental to a man's health and well-being.

I've not had to deal with the ordeal of proving my innocence during my twenty-six years of incarceration since I'm guilty of my crimes and entered prison acknowledging that I deserved to be here. I can't imagine being sent to hell if I hadn't done something so horrendous that it was justifiable. I've only encountered a few men in my circles that I really believed were innocent of the crime that brought them here. One of them is Glen Howard, whom I've had the privilege to befriend and work with as well as live in the same unit.

I've watched Glen over the course of these years battle the court system for his freedom. The process is a grueling ordeal that can make a man wonder if it is all worth it. Even before coming to prison Glen waited three years for his trial to begin which made it difficult to maintain a job to pay for the lawyers that were needed to prove his innocence. When someone is accused of a crime, whether guilty or not, it doesn't take long for friends and even some family, to head off into the sunset. Often the person being charged with a crime has to endure the battle alone or mostly alone. Between the expenses it takes on the purse as well as the emotional expense, it becomes too heavy on those around him.

I asked Glen about that day in September of 2013, the day his two-week trial ended and his verdict was read, he commented:

> Everything was in slow motion, so much was going through my mind. I knew that the verdict should be "innocent," but felt in my gut it was not going to be right. When the judge said "guilty"—and told the bailiff to take me into custody, I was emotionless, frozen, in total disbelief, and soon I began to fear what was going to happen to me. The court officer, whom I had known for more than ten years, had treated me kindly and professionally throughout the process, until that verdict was read. He immediately began treating me with disgust, as if I had lost all of my humanity at a particular moment in time.

Being handcuffed and walked out of court to begin his prison sentence was not something Glen ever imagined doing. He was a graduate of the Criminal Justice Academy, a military man, trained as an emergency medical technician, a public servant who had a great respect for the law and loved protecting and caring for people. Now he was beginning a fifty-year prison sentence along with thousands of convicted felons, gang members, and lots of people who would wish him harm due to his charges.

Glen's initiation was brutal—beatings, sexual assaults, and everything terrible one can endure in prison and still live, he experienced. Even now, after years have passed, Glen has trouble talking about those early days. He told me that his brain couldn't accept what was happening because it seemed so illogical that he was being faced with so much torment when he was an innocent man. In fact, he said:

> I hid all the horrible things going on from those around
> me because I didn't want to face the repercussions of ap-
> pearing weak and even more vulnerable. I almost have to
> forget that I don't belong here—because otherwise, anger
> and frustration takes over and becomes emotionally de-
> structive. Working hard at my job and staying focused on
> the work, helps to keep my mind from remembering that
> I am in prison and all that I have lost.

It took Glen a few years to build a community of friends where such attacks would finally end. The mental and physical stress he faced, caused great depression and anxiety that created a need for medication for high blood pressure and the lack of sufficient mental health assistance, left him to deal with his other troubles by himself.

The amazing compassion Glen has towards those around him is beautiful to witness. On many occasions I have watched him come to the aid of someone in the middle of a medical emergency. While the person in need is waiting on medical personnel to respond, he quickly jumps in and offers care and aid, when others simply don't know what to do. He talks to everyone and is genuinely concerned with their needs and has an empathetic ear due to his own struggles with life and the courts.

It takes a special stamina to fight your case in court once you've come to prison. As far as society, the courts, and just about everyone else, you are guilty and deserve whatever befalls you. If you do not have money to hire a private attorney, you almost have to become a jailhouse lawyer yourself to get any paperwork into the courts for consideration. The prison system does not make it easy to get the things you need to battle for your freedom—from get-ting to the law library, the copies of law you need, the addresses of where paperwork needs to be filed, finding a Notary to witness your signature, and saving up the postage to send the documents—it's all navigating a rocky sea in unknown waters.

If one is so fortunate to get any consideration from the courts, the ordeal of getting to court is an amazing endurance rivaling an Olympic competition. This is where Glen finds himself—going to court to try and get evidence entered that was not done so at his trial. Glen has traveled to court on three occasions since coming to prison. To accomplish this, he has spent eighty-four days away from his assigned prison site, and only about ten minutes in an actual court room just one time. The other two times he never made it past the county jail where he was housed for his court date.

The process of leaving the prison and going to court is a grueling one. Glen describes the experience:

> In the middle of the night, an officer wakes you up and tells you to pack your stuff. You put all your belongings in trash bags that are stored in the prison's property room. More than likely, some, if not all of your property will be stolen or misplaced. You wait in a cramped small cell in the prison processing area for hours, until the chain bus arrives to pick you up. Shackles are placed on your feet and hands and you sit on hard benches on the bus with a toilet in the very back. You are pressed up against the person beside you like sardines in a small can. When you finally get to the prison you realize that your journey is not over. From there you still have to travel from the prison site to the county jail where your court appearance is to be. While there you are placed in segregation and stay in your cell twenty-three hours a day, only out for a shower. All of this for a few minutes in front on the Judge, if you are lucky. When you get back to your home prison, weeks later, you end up in a strange cell, maybe with the job you left, hopefully some of your property intact, but exhausted, wondering if you are able to endure the next time.

This process can wear even the most fit person down to a willingness to plea or settle on something far from an exoneration agreement. There are hundreds of guys in prison working on their cases and trying to get some relief from the courts. Howard's is unusual in that he is claiming he is totally innocent of the crimes he is charged with and therefore, settling for anything other than a complete exoneration would be a major compromise if he ever was offered such a chance in the court system.

I often see Howard lost in thought and wonder what he must be thinking. I would imagine he is looking around at the surroundings of the hell he is in and imaging how he got there. It would be easy for a person to crawl up in a ball and cry himself to death and feel like the world has abandoned him. But Howard has chosen the more difficult route, of facing the monster that is trying to keep him in bondage, and trying to slay the dragon that is eating him alive. Let's pray his sword remains sharp and pointed.

> **TWEET:**
> We fight for change because we love. We believe in "impossible dreams" because we love. Our faith calls us not to simply visit the prisoner, but to set the captives free, and thereby set ourselves free.

My Prayer Today: Lord, take hold of my mind, my
body, my emotions today—my skin seems too thin
to bear the weight of negativity coming my way. I
need your protection from those around me, from
myself, and most of all from what my mind can
come up with.

CHANGE

I have been blessed most of my days in prison to have people in
my life to provide wisdom, advice, and rays of hope and understanding when I find myself in the pit. Recently, a good friend of
mine, Terrance Heard, and I were speaking about how a person can
change while in prison, and when he does change, if all his work is
in vain when it comes to society. "Big Heard," as I call him, since he
is an imposing figure, that carries the gravitas of a seasoned min-
ister and the respect from convicts on every side of the spectrum,
has changed right in front of my eyes. Years and years ago, I knew
Big Heard at the first prison I was housed. At that time, he was a
gang banger who participated in all the things you might suspect a
banger would. I did not have a good impression of him and in fact,
was quite intimidated by his presence, so I avoided him at all costs.
Now, years later, I find myself at the same prison with Big Heard,
where he has grown into one of the loveliest, gentle souls, who has
an incredibly compassionate heart. In fact, he has led a church

service here for some time, which is the largest attended service at the facility. Now, after all this time, we find ourselves friends. I wanted Big Heard to comment on "change" and what he thought that meant to the person changing and the people watching the change occur. Here are his thoughts:

Big Heard:

> Underneath the pretentious veneer of every human being exists a remarkable appetite to be somebody. Despite demographics, geography or social distinctions you will find a common yearn for a reality beyond our current experience. Not only do we flirt with the prospect of change but deep down we know we need to. What is true for most people on the fence, is that much of what we hope to be in this life only comes to us by way of self-change. Simple enough, though this fact is not realized without the precious aid of discontentment. It is not enough to say, "I want something different for my life" and then fail to take necessary steps to secure the path to be different. In essence, the notion that we can change our lives without changing ourselves is false.
>
> In my own experience with change I endured a grueling confrontation with self and the recourse to be a different person. I would venture to say this experience is not unique, but most people who are honest with the process of change found it difficult to lay down principles and oddities that were instinctively a part of their personality. Particularly for me, a life style of gang banging, drug dealing, and pointless chugging, allowed its legitimacy through a superficial worldview that played into the common grievance of a minority social caste. I bought into the thinking that urban communities don't have much of a choice. Inevitably, that same lifestyle yoked me into a criminal scenario which ultimately placed me in a prison.
>
> Having little to no resources to aid in any immediate relief, my worldview was put under serious question. As life faded around me, the very weight of this experience baring down upon my shoulders drove me to my knees. However, it was not prison alone that buckled me,

but more so what prison revealed about myself and that world in which I identified with. Without warning I became disillusioned and burdened with the responsibility to make a quality decision about my life. Finally, I could appreciate the benefit of purposefully engaging the issues of my life rather than responding to life as it came to me. Fortunately for humanity, the empowerment to change can be found in various places; but, specifically for me, it was my faith in Christ that brought perspective to my broken life. As a result, I am careful to point out that until a person comes to the end of self, you will never truly morph into someone new, nor could you enjoy the benefits of a new life.

What would happen if the world acknowledged the truth about the power of change? The fact it is very real and accessible undermine the legitimacy of writing people off and closing the door to restoration. The conflict, so it seems, is those who acknowledge the power of change must acquiesce to redemption; otherwise, change could not be genuinely celebrated. More to the point, when people change for the better they anticipate the reward of new beginnings and also the affirmation. When this reward is missing from the equation the big picture becomes blurred and often times thwart the momentum in the process. This is especially true for men and women who are incarcerated, who stand naked without the slightest benefit of the doubt. One of the great tragedies of my generation is witnessing the so called civilized nation stand aloof and unaffected by any change in those who are incarcerated. Consequently, society makes little to no investment in the process, neither in their policies, programs or social networking.

Assuming our nation of laws still champion the notion of rehabilitation, I fear we have lost that priority in our thirst for vengeance; if this is true, then we all have some changing of our own to do. If history is any guide, then let us remember how those who successfully challenged the status quo prevailed by pushing their issues to the forefront of national politics. But, if our society sleeps on this issue, we could never qualify the proverbial notion of rehabilitation.

> **TWEET:**
> I don't expect the entire criminal system is going
> to be abolished in my lifetime. There were
> people fighting before me, people fighting now,
> and there will be people fighting for it after me.
> We must do what we can in our space of life.

Being in prison is like being a dog at the humane society, without the *humane* aspect of it.

—Jeff S. Noland

HUMANE

My cellee and I were watching TV when a commercial came on showing dogs and cats that had been mistreated, abandoned and now caged while waiting their fates. Dramatic and gut-wrenching music played as one picture after another popped on the screen, making my heart cry. My cellee commented, "Being in prison is like being a dog at the humane society, without the *humane* aspect of it." I nodded my head in agreement and suddenly found myself getting angry. The feeling caught me off guard and didn't seem to match the circumstances. I finally interpreted the anger as actually being jealousy. Imagine my confusion when I concluded I was jealous of a pitiful puppy I saw locked in the cage on television.

I love animals and certainly don't want to see any harmed or mistreated. Caging an animal after I have been caged for twenty-six years is something I could never do. I had to dig a little bit to find the basis of my jealousy. So what did the dog have that I didn't?

a. A national campaign to fight for his life and happiness.
b. Movie stars and famous singers advocating for his release and adoption.

c. Millions of dollars being spent to help him and other animals from being harmed or mistreated.

d. The realization by society that his life, all animal life, is important and deserves to be treasured and not killed or abused. No more "Kill Shelters" just "Adoption Agencies."

Maybe instead of being jealous of Fido, I need to be inspired by him. If society can change its perspective on the humane treatment of pets, then, could it also do so for humans in locked cages behind bars—maybe even those on death row? Perhaps those of us who are requesting legitimate prison reform need to do a better job of sharing the stories of those incarcerated, their repentance, their worth to the community.

So with my new found inspiration, I have decided that our campaign needs some painful pictures of pitiful prisoners who have been beaten and robbed by violent gang members, and some other stories of medical patients left in a cold, steel room dying of cancer with nothing more than a Tylenol for pain. And we will need some heart-warming stories of inmates who have served twenty or thirty years and have done everything asked of them by the parole board, and yet are being told "Denied parole for seriousness of offense." I will even provide the first testimonial for the commercial:

> Hi, I'm Tony Vick. I've been locked up for twenty-six years for terrible things I did. I'm not the same person now that I was then. If you come to see me, you might just discover that I am a warm, caring person that is a good friend. I deserved to come to prison, but I'm not so sure I deserved to be assaulted, robbed, raped and dehumanized since arriving. I am a broken man whose body is about given out, but I want to leave this world with something better than I gave it when I was free. If you will provide me a safe home, even if it's behind this razor wire, I will be extremely grateful and will do everything in my power to help those around me.

What I've learned from Fido is that my job is to show the ugly pictures and tell the stories that are hard to hear if I ever want society to understand that life in prison is not life at all; it is a daily struggle for survival. Glossing over the ugliness only perpetuates the status quo. And that is not okay.

TWEET:

We don't touch in prison—an imaginary wall is put up between us where it's a sin to invade the personal spaces. I miss it! At times I feel like I have the plague and people are dammed if they touch me. I wonder if I will be like a scared cat if ever free again?

THE BIG SIXTY

This morning I accidentally glanced at the steel plate attached above the sink that substitutes for an actual mirror that would be a security risk in prison. I usually avoid such confrontations since my twenty-six years in prison have taken a toll on my hair, skin and general disposition. But this morning, on my sixtieth birthday, I took a gander at this strange old man staring back at me. He couldn't take his eyes off of mine, as though he was as surprised as I was to see what I looked like and that I had taken the time to stop and, not just to look, but to see. I settled into the experience and planted my feet solidly on the floor, and decided it was time to gauge this face, this body, and this soul to determine what was left and what to do with what remained.

I must tell you, it wasn't a pretty sight. This strange man had weary eyes, as though he had seen many horrific things through the years that must have taken a toll on him. His skin was weathered and wrinkly like worry has been his best friend for decades. His hair was scarce and gray from regret and wisdom gained from reflection over bad decisions, wrong paths taken, and hurt he caused so many. The man had the audacity to tear up. What was he crying for—he was in the mirror? The tears rolled, not for sadness over the old image in the steel plate, but for all the people who has loved him, who he disappointed, who he hurt, who he killed. Why is he still alive —so underserved to be breathing air, to exist at all?

It's senseless to complain about the hardships of prison when I feel so deserving to be there. If I didn't believe in God and the mercy he bestows on his children, I would be at a complete loss. It's easy to tell others about God's mercy and forgiveness, but it is harder to accept it for yourself. I must continually remind myself that talking to God is essential to the health of my psyche and a balm to my soul. I guess that is also why I feel the need to write about prison and the reform needed within these walls. Most of the incarcerated will get out one day, and I pray that they will be transformed while behind these steel walls. That they will walk back into a community that offers them mercy and an opportunity for redemption. So as much as the insiders need to look in the mirror, so to, must the outsiders.

When I look in the mirror, I don't want to see wasted days, wasted years, wasted decades —then, all of a sudden, a wasted life. I'm in prison, so I must start here to make myself, the situation, and the world better. Otherwise, the conclusion to my story will be a wasted life. So I am calling on all believers of God and his redemptive power of mercy and forgiveness to examine their thoughts on those we incarcerate in America. Mercy must replace revenge, and kindness must replace hate. It's a rough trail for all of us to tread— but we must travel it together, or we are all doomed to destroy one another. Life, wherever you find it, is worth something, is redeemable, is valuable, is loved by God—and therefore must be by us.

> **TWEET:**
> All the flowers in my garden are in snapshots
> cataloged in my memory. Occasionally,
> though, the wind brings me a teasing scent of
> sweet yesteryear, and my heart sings.

IT'S OKAY TO NOT BE OKAY

I'm really having to fight that feeling of going deep inside myself, turning out the lights, and sitting in the corner with my thumb in my mouth. It feels like my tiny box is getting smaller and smaller, and breath is harder and harder to achieve. I simply want to be able to expand my lungs to full capacity with some sort of air that doesn't have the stench of prison crap.

Further acerbating this negativity is the incompetent prison staff I see wasting resources, manpower and time. It's like they have been given all the ingredients to make a soufflé, but all they can produce are mud pies. Last night, yet another officer walked out in tears in fear. He was simply trying to keep gang members from other units entering the unit he was assigned. As a result, the gang members told him to leave or be killed—so he left. He had no back-up and no defense mechanisms other than a radio to call for help. Before help could have arrived, it would have all been over. Inmates have even less defense resources to protect themselves from gang violence—so most are open prey to the whims of gangs.

Prison administration treat their own front line staff as terribly as the inmates. It's no wonder that most staff do not treat the insiders humanely—when they are not being treated humanely by those in charge of their safety. This all trickles down to a dysfunctional mess that is violent and chaotic; a place that insiders or outsiders do not want to be and certainly cannot entertain any type of rehabilitation for the offenders. Living in the midst of constant violence without any sense that the people in charge are, in fact, in charge, can weather away at your spirit.

How much can my mind, body, and soul endure before they all just give up? I keep reaching new thresholds that I never thought possible when entertaining that question. I keep demanding myself to get over it, to be okay. The best I can do is simply acknowledge that it is okay to not be okay. I can make that decision and stick to it.

> **TWEET:**
> No matter how deeply I sink into the dark pit
> of despair, my God is there with a flickering
> candle, reminding me to bring him closer,
> closer, closer. He's jealous of our time together.

THE ABSENTEE

Oh Lord, be with those that love me today—for they
have paid harshly for their love. As you gave your life
for my life, so have these people given their well-
being for me. Their love brings me hope, presents me
with your hugs wrapped tightly around me when all
else seems hopeless. Help me to love as you love me.

The first time my parents came to visit me in prison all we did was cry and look at each other. There were not any words needed to convey what we were feeling. That was decades ago and the emotions associated with that visit still haunt me today. I understood that day that my parents had been sentenced also—to a lifetime of pain, shame and abandonment. They were kicked out of their retirement community due to the media being camped out on the property wanting comments from them. My brother stopped speaking to them because they would not disown me, and they were shunned by most of their friends and family. They received a harsher sentence than me because they had done nothing wrong. My son who was just ten at the time, had to live with them, and there they were, two retired seniors—parents once again to a young boy. My son has grown up with all the struggles associated with his father being in prison—the situations he has had to endure astonish me and breaks my heart. My parents and brother are all dead now, and I imagine that all the pain I caused them led to early graves.

My friend, Charlie is going through all of these emotions right now. I asked him to write a few words about this subject:

Charles:

> What words come to mind when you think of an inmate living in prison? I am sure that they are similar to the words that have been used to describe myself ever since, as a twenty-one-year-old kid in the year 2014, I committed the terrible act of murder: criminal, felon, menace, terror, crook, offender, transgressor, evildoer, lawbreaker, etc. For those of us who are guilty that sit in prison today, these titles are justly placed upon our heads. There are people and families in society that we have wronged who rightly consider us in the manner of that terminology. It only makes sense that we are removed from close proximity to them, so peaceful living may be sought by them.
>
> For a moment, I would like to direct your attention to another set of families: ours. Take mine, for example: middle class Christians, living in small town Tennessee, making the most of every possible moment in life, together. Then, one of their bonehead members commits murder. Understandably so, a torrential shock disturbed their routine of living, leaving them baffled and confused.
>
> Those terms may very well have crossed their minds concerning myself, but an amazing and awesome love prevailed. They have been by my side through the entire criminal justice process. For my family, since my conviction and incarceration occurred, a different term is used to define my place amongst them: absent.
>
> At beautiful holiday dinners, no plate is prepared for me; my seat remains empty. I am the elephant-in-the-room at the family vacations, and never present to celebrate joyous and prominent moments in their individual lives. My family has confided in me that this is painful for them. The vacancy I left behind is felt as a stressful ache in their hearts as they adjust to life missing a beloved member.

Learning this has led me to ponder the vast number of families in society who are experiencing the same sadness mine is feeling. Those terms mentioned previously need not be extended from us to them. We made our own choice to put a stain upon our family name. Our own families are most certainly victimized by what we have done to end up in prison. The major difference in their victimization is that, in almost all cases, families will stick together to struggle alongside one another as their love and devotion, ingrained in shared DNA, overrides the pain of wrongdoing.

Has this struggle ever crossed your mind when your thoughts fell on prisoners? Honestly, as a free man in society, it never settled into my brain. I looked right over it, never seeing until experiencing it myself.

Several men that I have met in prison were the financial foundation of their family, their loved ones now struggle alone, forced to overexert to stay afloat. Some were caretakers to handicapped or ailing kin, regularly performing tasks around home and running errands their hindered relatives could not. Definitely, the majority of us incarcerated peoples left behind a group of individuals, large or small, who now mingle with the absentee, the specter that lingers amongst them as a constant reminder that they are no longer whole.

Now, my eyes are open to the need within these families. The vacancy is an uncomfortable emptiness, but could be combated with someone willing to simply be there, to stand in whatever moment is needed, to offer words of encouragement, or a listening ear to those who are lonely, stressed and at the end of their rope. There is a need for support, for motivation, for love, for a presence to aid in the absent spaces.

> **TWEET:**
> No matter how lonely you are, rain still falls on the ground outside your window—looking at earth that you cannot tread, but only dream of.

WITNESS

Learning to adapt to the accepted prison norms expected from fellow inmates and staff can be taxing on one's conscience. This typically means walking in oblivion to what's going on around you. Doing otherwise, could quickly get you killed. There are not many one-on-one confrontations anymore where you have a beef, have a fist-fight and then it's over. Now, it's all about the gangs and they run in packs. Mess with one of them, and you have twenty of them trying to kill you with homemade shanks. For instance, this week alone I have witnessed the following:

a. An officer was held up at knife point by a gang of three in-mates—they demanded his watch.
b. An officer was pushed to the ground when trying to defend the security of the fence gate giving access in and out of the unit.
c. A gang robbed and beat up several people after they received their weekly commissary.

Witnessing such acts of violence is commonplace in prison, at least at this one for now. Staff and inmates are left to fend for themselves because the prison is short-staffed and out of control. The gangs have taken over the prison—domestic terrorists. The thought of going to the rec yard or to church or other programs seems absurd at this point, not only are there no staff to run such things, but if there were it would not be safe to do so. The state prison system has allowed the gangs to build up such power, numbers, and prestige within these walls, that it will take a major change to secure the facility to an environment that will attract a staff willing to work. So what could be done quickly and have immediate results:

a. Put inmates who are classified the same in the same unit. Example: Inmates who have been classed as minimum security because they have followed the rules should live together. Likewise, those that are classified at medium security because of infractions while incarcerated, should be housed together. It's not rocket science—but one would think that it was when dealing with government bureaucrats.

That's the whole kit and caboodle, just "A" needed, all else would take care of itself. No extra money needed, no increase in the budget, just a little moving around within the prison. After that, the prison could arrange its staff where it is needed the most—simply good management of your resources.

The key to the entire scenario of prison improvement requires a simple change in the view about the souls inside the razor wire— *We Are Human Beings*—not livestock that is tagged and owned by masters who just want to make a profit. Many care more about how their chickens and cows live prior to butchering them than they do their fellow humans beings. If the community wants inmates to become good organic men and women who are capable of living in the free fields of life again, it must start with believing that all people, even those incarcerated, are due *humane* treatment.

> ## TWEET:
> I heard two guards telling us insiders, "These guys aren't normal, they're animals in a zoo." To which I thought in my head, "The only normal people you know are the ones you don't know very well." Luckily, this time, my mouth stayed shut.

TWEET:
If America wants a death penalty, it should be in the public square or on TV for all to see. You shouldn't get to hide in the safety of your house and not watch what you are promoting. There are plenty of people in prison who were only spectators at a murder and found culpable.

THE HISTORY OF KILLING PEOPLE FOR JUSTICE

As of October 2021, the United States had 2,455 people on death row, with California having most at 695. The number of people under sentence of death in the US has fallen below 2,500 for the first time in twenty-nine years following twenty consecutive years of decline, according to the US Department of Justice Bureau of Justice Statistics. The amount of time prisoners have been on death row approaches nineteen years on average. Just watching news stories and hearing Americans talk about a person who has committed a murder, it would seem that the majority of Americans favor the death penalty. So how did we get to this point? Let's take a look at the history of killing people for justice.

From ancient times until well into the nineteenth century, many societies administered exceptionally cruel forms of capital punishment. In Rome the condemned were hurled from the Tarpeian Rock; for murdering a close relative they were drowned in a sealed bag with a dog, cock, ape, and viper; and still others were executed by forced gladiatorial combat or by crucifixion. Executions in ancient China were carried out by many painful methods, such as sawing the condemned in half, flaying him while still alive, and boiling. Cruel forms of execution in Europe included "breaking" on the wheel, boiling in oil, burning at the stake, decapitation by the guillotine or an axe, hanging, drawing and quartering, and drowning. Although by the end of the twentieth century many jurisdictions (e.g., nearly every US state that employs the death penalty, Guatemala, the Philippines, Taiwan, and some Chinese provinces) had adopted lethal injection, offenders continued to be beheaded in Saudi Arabia and occasionally stoned to death (for adultery) in Iran and the Sudan.

Other methods of execution were electrocution, gassing, and the firing squad. Historically, executions were public events, attended by large crowds, and the mutilated bodies were often displayed until they rotted. Public executions were banned in England in 1868, though they continued to take place in parts of the United States until the 1930s. In the last half of the twentieth century, there was considerable debate regarding whether executions should be broadcast on televisions, as has occurred in Guatemala.

Since the mid-1990s public executions have taken place in some twenty countries, including Iran, Saudi Arabia, and Nigeria, though the practice has been condemned by the United Nations Human Rights Committee as "incompatible with human dignity." In many countries death sentences are not carried out immediately after they are imposed; there is often a long period of uncertainty for the convicted while their cases are appealed. Inmates awaiting execution live on what has been called *death row*; in the United States and Japan, some prisoners have been executed more than fifteen years after their convictions. The European Union regards this phenomenon as so inhumane that, on the basis of a binding ruling by the European Court of Human Rights (1989), European Union countries may extradite an offender accused of a capital crime to a country that practices capital punishment only if a guarantee is given that the death penalty will not be sought.

ARGUMENTS FOR AND AGAINST CAPITAL PUNISHMENT

Capital punishment has long engendered considerable debate about both its morality and its effect on criminal behavior. Contemporary arguments for and against capital punishment fall under three general headings: moral, utilitarian, and practical.

Moral Arguments

Supporters of the death penalty believe that those who commit murder, because they have taken the life of another, have forfeited their own right to life. Furthermore, they believe, capital punishment is a just form of retribution, expressing and reinforcing the moral indignation not only of the victim's relatives but of law-abiding citizens in general. By contrast, opponents of capital punishment, argue that, by legitimizing the very behavior that the law seeks to repress—killing—capital punishment is counterproductive in the moral message it conveys. Moreover, they urge, when it is used for lesser crimes, capital punishment is immoral because it is wholly disproportionate to the harm done. Abolitionists also claim that capital punishment violates the condemned person's right to life and is fundamentally inhuman and degrading. Although death was prescribed for crimes in many sacred religious documents and historically was practiced widely with the support of religious hierarchies, today there is no agreement among religious faiths, or among denominations or sects within them, on the morality of capital punishment. Beginning in the last half of the twentieth century, increasing numbers of religious leaders—particularly within Judaism and Roman Catholicism—campaigned against it. Capital punishment was abolished by the state of Israel for all offenses except treason and crimes against humanity, and Pope John Paul II condemned it as "cruel and unnecessary."

Utilitarian Arguments

Supporters of capital punishment also claim that it has a uniquely potent deterrent effect on potentially violent offenders for whom the threat of imprisonment is not a sufficient restraint. Opponents, however, point to research that generally has demonstrated that the death penalty is not a more effective deterrent than the alternative sanction of life or long-term imprisonment.

Practical Arguments

There also are disputes about whether capital punishment can be administered in a manner consistent with justice. Those who support capital punishment believe that it is possible to fashion laws and procedures that ensure that only those who are really deserving of death are executed. By contrast, opponents maintain that the historical application of capital punishment shows that any attempt to single out certain kinds of crime as deserving of death will inevitably be arbitrary and discriminatory. They also point to other factors that they think preclude the possibility that capital punishment can be fairly applied, arguing that the poor and ethnic and religious minorities often do not have access to good legal assistance, that racial prejudice motivates predominantly white juries in capital cases to convict black and other nonwhite defendants in disproportionate numbers, and that, because errors are inevitable even in a well-run criminal justice system, some people will be executed for crimes they did not commit. Finally, they argue that, because the appeals process for death sentences is protracted, those condemned to death are often cruelly forced to endure long periods of uncertainty about their fate.

TIMELINE OF US EXECUTION METHODS

Hanging

The noted method of execution in the US until the mid-twentieth century.

Electrocution

First adopted in 1888 in New York as a quicker and more humane alternative to hanging; 1890: New York electrocuted William Kemmier at Auburn State Prison; Martha Place became the first woman to be electrocuted; 1949: Electrocution was the method in twenty-six states; Between 1890–1972, 4,251 people were electrocuted.

Gas Chamber

Adopted in 1921 in Nevada to provide a more humane form of capital punishment than electrocution. By 1955, eleven states used the gas chamber. Between 1921–1972, six hundred people were put to death by gas.

Lethal Injection

Now the most widely used method of execution in the US first adopted in Oklahoma in 1977 because it was considered cheaper and more humane than electrocution or lethal gas. Texas was the first state to administer lethal injection, executing Charles Brooks on December 2, 1982.

While editor of the *Maximum Times,* a prison newspaper, I interviewed two inmates who began their sentences on death row. Both of these men are now free and living productive and meaningful lives in the freeworld. These personal accounts are from when these men were still fighting for their freedom:

William Murphy had over twenty years of prison under his belt and spent his first two and a half years on Tennessee's death row. Eventually, through the court system, his sentence was changed to a life sentence. However, it did take the court six months to properly complete the paperwork in order for him to be taken out of Riverbend's Unit Two (Death Row). Murphy stated that death row has step down levels. When the inmate first enters he is labeled as a Level C, which is like being on maximum security. After a considerable amount of time without incidents, you are then moved to a Level B, then to a Level A, to finally a Level 1A, which is the least restrictive of the death row levels. With each level change you are allowed less restrictions that will eventually include contact visitations.

Surprisingly, Murphy found the staff respectful and helpful on death row in helping him to get acclimated to his surroundings. He was especially impressed with most of the death row inmates who went out of their way to help him feel comfortable and informed about life in Unit Two. Murphy was also touched by the number of volunteers who gave of their time day after day to reach out to the inmates. Murphy commented that he is personally opposed to the death penalty and stated:

> It simply doesn't bring the closure for the victim's family that they think that it will. Plus, there is no evidence that it helps to lower the crime rates whatsoever. It seems that many people have that eye for an eye mentality and they simply want revenge. I think that if people would actually come to a prison and visit some of these guys on death row and see their humanity and look them eye to eye, that they would not be so inclined to wish death on them. Obviously nothing can change their crime, but that doesn't mean that their hearts can't be changed.

Ndume Olatushani, had this to say about his experience on death row:

> The whole process of being sentenced to death can be a daunting experience. Once I was thrown into a death cell left to try and figure out what it all meant on my own, this was sometimes overwhelming. I can't say there is such a thing as a "typical" day spent on death row, there were many days I didn't know what I was going to do. I know that everyone's experience is different even though the men and women on death row face the same possible fate. Living on death row is like living in a concrete bubble, you never walk more than fifty feet straight without having to turn left, right or turn back around to go back to your death cell. A trip out of the building was a welcomed one for me, because it gave me the chance to life outside of the bubble for a fleeting time. You never get to experience the sun shining on you unobstructed because you are in a cage—a cage that would be considered inhumane if used on any animal in the zoo. I spent twenty years never being able to walk on grass or be outside after dark where I could look up and see the stars in the sky. These examples may seem like insignificant things and we take them for granted. However, when these simple pleasures of life are taken away from us, we are denied a part of our humanity.
>
> The first time I was being escorted to the infirmary after landing on death row, shackled and chained as if I were a fictional monster brought to life, one of the officer's looked out the "peep hole" of this otherwise solid steel door

leading outside—banged on it with his nightstick, waited a few seconds and then he opened the door. He stepped out before me and shouted "Dead Man Walking!" In that instance I had this sobering moment that felt almost like it was happening in slow motion. And the whole time I was thinking: I am alive and I intended to keep it that way. At that point, I had not been outside for nearly a month. I was squinting my eyes trying to adjust them to the bright sunlight, and I could see all the other prisoners stop what they were doing and begin to clear a wide path as we made our way through. The only other experience that made every one stop what they were doing quicker was when the officers fired their high powered assault rifles, without the warning of a whistle—which meant someone had either been shot and wounded or worse killed.

There is nothing innate in the human experience that lets us know when we are supposed to depart from this earth. Being told the exact time, date, place and method in which we are going to die is unnatural. I wanted to live, the truly important things in life started coming into view with clarity. I was now ready to embrace life with invigoration in that "valley in the shadow of death." At the time I didn't know anything to do other than immerse myself in the law. I knew if I was going to escape the electrical voltage that the judge had prescribed when he pronounced my sentence of death, I had to learn about the laws that had put me there, so many of my days were spent in law books. While doing time on death row I really did find life because it allowed me plenty of time to assess my life and more importantly realize what the most important things are in life. Unfortunately, I think many people go through life searching for what they believe is their grand purpose, while never understanding that life has purpose. All we have to do is live our lives trying to be the best person that we can and the rest will take care of itself. The truth is it doesn't matter where we may find ourselves mired down in the mud holes of life, great people and things have been forged in the face of adversity. Beautiful flowers grow out of mud.

I couldn't draw a crooked line straight, but while I was sitting on death row I taught myself how to draw and paint. Some people think that I am a fairly accomplished artist—I have had my work shown in many places in this country and in a few other countries. I currently have three paintings that are touring the world along with several other inmates from around the country. Our work is accompanying a documentary dealing with the "hope and redemption" to be found in the two million plus of us men, women and children that are imprisoned today.

We all possess something special no matter where we are in life. This is one of the profound life lessons that gave me a new perspective on life, while on death row. I will offer this in closing, you don't have to go to death row to find life, we only have to embrace it right here right now. We have to make our minds up now because the fact is ninety-five percent of those of us here in prison will one day be going home. I don't know about the next man, but I am getting prepared to go out there and to live. Perhaps the phrase "Dead Man Walking" can be applied to any one of us here in prison. Is this living? I have often told people, that I didn't begin to live until I was actually faced with the prospect of death.

Whichever side of the argument that you fall on regarding putting people to death for their crimes, the facts bear out that many people who have been on death row have had their sentences changed, reduced, or dropped altogether, like the two men above. With the possibility that there may be innocent people facing death, what is the correct way forward? It seems Americans are slowly changing their opinions about this matter, but will it be in time to save the lives of the 2,455 people facing death right now? Statistics demonstrate, that some of those will be found innocent. Are we willing to take the chance of putting an innocent person to death?

> **TWEET:**
> When humans are warehoused with no chance for restoration to their community, and are of more economic value locked in a cage than free, that is slavery. The only moral response to slavery is abolition.

TWEET:

Holy Spirit

hoovering over my soul

cleansing my vessel

from wounds, mistakes,

Stay with me

just for a while

Let me feel your comfort, your peace

just for a while

Then I'll release you back to

the angels, until next time we visit.

MY SON

My son Jonathon, was ten years old when I came to prison. He has had a difficult time with the realization that his father was capable of committing murder. In 2015, he sent me a paper he had written about our relationship. He doesn't speak to me anymore, but occasionally I get the paper out that he sent to me and read it. It helps me to remember that perhaps there is still love in his heart for me. And if so, that is a merciful and miraculous blessing.

From Jonathon:

> One of the hardest aspects of my life to explore is my relationship with my father. I looked up to him as my hero when I was a child, so his betrayals were earth shattering for me. Ever since he went to prison, he has written several times a year trying to rebuild our bonds as father and son. Looking back, he probably only considered me an important object or possession when he was free, but after years of being in prison I believe he finally accepted who he was and perhaps now genuinely cares for me as his son.
>
> There were times where I hated him so much, but now I only hate his actions of the past. He often asked

me for forgiveness, but that is something I don't think I can ever offer. I'm hesitant to develop our relationship any further than short talks and letters because doing so would be like forgiving his transgressions; some things in life can't be taken back. Even though I can't forgive him, I am still proud of some of the things he has accomplished while in prison. Many people with life sentences give up and are no longer productive individuals, but he teaches people and sometimes helps others in similar situations.

All people, even those doomed to spend their life in prison can still be of use to society. No matter how small the contribution, what you did in the past doesn't matter if you can help even one person regain hope or deal with their demons. Only by accepting who we are can we hope to truly live a meaningful life. Accepting who you are doesn't mean accepting everything about your life or situation because there are always parts we can improve. Don't give up on yourself just because of temporary hardships or pain, remember that others have gone through worse and still managed to live inspirational lives. This life is all we have, so as long as we are still living we should constantly struggle to improve and help others. When I die, I want the world to be better because of me.

> **TWEET:**
> What would you do if you weren't afraid?
> I'd write the story I've never told anyone, the
> one that only lives in my mind.

TWEET:

I'm not who I was twenty-six years ago I'm not
who I was yesterday
Today I plan to be different still. I'm fickle and
precious deal with it!

SPEAKING TRUTH MATTERS

Over a decade ago, I was involved in a prison organization that spoke to high school and college students who visited the prison. (PAIICE: Prisoners Actively Involved In Community Education) The purpose wasn't to scare them to death but to speak on how we got to where we were and perhaps point out the things in our lives that had been our greatest mistakes. After each of us convicts delivered our speeches, we exited the room and never got to interact with the students. My speech included how being dishonest about my sexual identity and keeping it hidden from everyone, was the catalyst to all my transgressions leading to prison. My intent was to express how important truth is to being able to live authentically and happily.

The staff sponsor of the organization was Charles Chadwick and one afternoon he brought me a note from Louise C. that he had received in the mail. It read as follows:

> May 10, 2009
> Dear Mr. Chadwick,
>
> I wish to thank you and the PAIICE Organization for my grandson's life. Yes, I did say life. Recently he came with his class to a presentation at your prison. Soon afterwards he came to spend the weekend with me to help me plant my garden beds. I could tell immediately that he was much happier than I had seen him in months. There was a sparkle in his eyes that had been missing. After a long day outside, we sat and talked. He opened up to me like never before. He told me about his recent trip to your prison. He said that just prior he had decided to kill

himself, and that he was resolute in his decision. He told me of the men who spoke to him, some were murderers, drug dealers, and some convicted wrongly. He said their stories made him feel like he could decide a different path. He particularly took heart to a story about a man in prison for killing his wife, who had kept the secret that he way gay for years and years. His religious upbringing prevented him from embracing his truth. I'm sorry that he did not remember the man's name. Our family did not know my grandson had been fighting the same secret that the inmate held. When he heard the man's story he realized that being honest was not the worst thing, that killing himself would destroy lots of lives. As a family, we have dealt with this and we are grateful to have our grandson with us. I cannot imagine how we would have survived if he had taken his life over a troubled heart.

Thank you for providing such a wonderful program. I wanted you to know the impact of it all. God bless you and the men at your prison who saved my grandson's life. We will be eternally grateful. And even though these inmates may have done bad things to get them there, praise God that they are now willing to reach out and help others. Surely God will bless them. We all discussed how we could repay you. We wanted to pass it on to someone else in need. So in the name of PAIICE, we donated $1,000 to the Suicide Prevention Program. Again, God Bless You All.

Louise C.

Also, my daughter had a great Mother's Day because of you.

TWEET:

Old Head Wisdom:

I spent a lot of years before prison lying about everything—which led me to this awful place.
One thing is for sure, if you tell the truth, it becomes a part of your past. If you lie, it becomes a part of your future.

TWEET:
When friends are released from prison
they always promise to write, help, etc.
The disappointment from that usually never
happening, lends me to tell those leaving, "Just
be happy, and think of me occasionally when
you are feeling loved, nourished and fulfilled."

MY CELLEE'S ABOUT TO BE FREE!

If you allow yourself to see past his charges, past his prison number, and look at him—really look, you will find an amazing, contrite and humble spirit that has used his ten years of incarceration in a manner that demonstrates his desire to be a good, honest and decent human being. Despite his many hard years in prison, despite all the obstacles put in his way, and despite the system that has erected multiple hurdles for him to clear, he is optimistic and very excited about re-entering the free world.

Jeff Noland, my cellee for some years now, is about to enter the free world. He has loving family members scattered across the country, friends who live in and out of the state of Tennessee, and has saved his money by working hard and putting every penny available aside for such a day. He has sought forgiveness from God, family, and everyone who is willing to read his words or take his calls. And in a few weeks he will have paid man's debt to society and his community for his crime.

He, like so many, have been placed on a lifetime register because of his crime. So he can only live in certain locations, work at certain places, and must pay fees and take classes for years and years. He will not be able to seek comfort at a church, or visit parks, or go to ballgames, or ever really be free. The determination for his future limited existence was given to him without any personal consideration—only because the law requires people receiving certain charges be under a blanket of rules and regulations. No psychologist, psychiatrist, or even a social worker, has any input into what type of supervision he may or may not need when he leaves prison. No value has been placed on the ten years of hard work or the changes he has toiled to make.

I understand the value in having such strict guidelines for some people leaving prison and keeping track of their habits and whereabouts. But by having such guidelines for everyone without individualized assessment puts a great expense to the taxpayers that is absolutely not necessary. In fact, having such blanketed guidelines inhibits the successful reintegration for so many who are desperately trying to simply live and survive after being released from prison.

Soon the money Jeff has saved for years will go for the monthly fees for an ankle bracelet, charges for unnecessary classes he must attend, and monthly monitoring fees that he must pay just because his crime falls into the category that says he must. The system has done something amazing for Jeff, *set him up for failure*. He still must find a job, money for an apartment and basic needs, transportation, clothes to wear to a job, and a way to secure medical insurance. That would have been a good use for that money he has been saving for years.

I've had many cellees over my twenty-six years of being in prison—but I have not encountered one who has done as much self-improvement as Jeff has, nor have I met a kinder, gentler spirit in this place. He loved God before coming to prison, has loved God through prison, and now prepares to serve God upon leaving prison—that is consistent God loving. He will need that love when he is released on August 29th—because the world awaiting him will be cruel. Sure, there will be some who embrace him, but the engine that we have built—The Criminal Justice Incarceration Machine— is well fueled to run him into the ground at every opportunity.

How do these injustices exist? The people that they affect, the incarcerated and those released are non-voting citizens which have no voice that matters to elected officials who are responsible for making laws. And people getting out of prison, many who will be on the life time register and supervision that Jeff will be on, do not have the luxury to advocate for change. Businesses don't typically hire folks who demonstrate with signs outside of the capitol, and landlords don't recruit ex-felons who will show up on electronic maps in a negative manner to their empty apartments. Finding a job and a place to live has to take priority over the luxury of demonstration against the injustices that exist.

Jeff, like so many being released, may have family and friends who would gladly provide him a place to live, even if temporarily. But the many restrictions placed on him makes many of those locations unacceptable. If someone is released that cannot find a living location acceptable to the state, the person is rendered homeless and taken to the county where they were convicted, and if they have money can check into a motel, if not, then they are on their own. It is a vicious cycle that we must come to terms with before everyone is trapped in a system that is impossible to ever be free from.

How to help Jeff and others leaving prison? If you have an apartment or house to rent, consider someone who is desperate to be a good citizen and will be loyal and caring for your place like Jeff will be. If you need a worker who has done ten years of hard time and has taken every improvement opportunity available and will be loyal and attentive to everything asked of him, then hire Jeff and give him a chance. If you have some decent clothes and start-up things he will need to survive, then pass them along. If you have a vehicle you do not need then consider allowing him to drive it to get back and forth to work. If you have a smile or a prayer or a handshake when he walks out those prison gates, then offer them to him.

Please take care of my dear friend, my brother—I'll never get to see him again, so I trust him into your care. Don't crush the man he is now, because he is a good man.

> ### TWEET:
> I've watched so many friends walk out of this prison, many times I help carry their stuff to the gate. Each time it's like seeing the ugliness of this place leave and imagining new hope developing. My heart withers with each departure, knowing I will never see them again.

DEPARTING

It had been a practice I had long surrendered to—my inability to not cry like a baby at such moments. The practice, that is, of helping my cellee, my friend, carry his property to intake in order to be processed out and released from prison. But in this case, I could not bear to give up any moment to see him, to be in his presence, before knowing I would never see him again.

We made it through the unit gate onto the prison yard—he glanced at me and I at him, purposely not holding a stare for more than a second. If we spoke words, I don't remember. I looked at him like I was painting a picture, his black hair, his broad shoulders, his long body, the gait of his walk and the timid excitement about his day, demonstrated by his slight quivering. My stomach was also jumping about—what should I say at this moment? It should be something profound so he will engrave it in his memory. My words failed me, and all I was able to muster was, "I love you." Trying to say one more word would have released the dam of emotion I was not prepared to swim through.

> **TWEET:**
> I watched from my prison window the sun
> set—falling behind the trees into the hills. I had
> to erase from my vision the razor wire that was
> placed before the picturesque painting God
> had sent me. It was a reminder that nothing man
> creates can separate you from the love of God.

PART TWO

The Aftermath of Prison Business

JEFF NOLAND

> **TWEET:**
> Every day, wherever we may be—we must choose to get up, get going and get things done. Life is not going to be brought to us on a silver platter lounging in bed. Some days may be better than others—but inch forward, not backwards—crawl or walk, doesn't matter.

LEAVING CAPTIVITY

1. Every year, more than half a million inmates are released from prison.
2. Nearly two thirds of those who are released will be arrested within three years.
3. Some of the most common problems facing former inmates are the difficulty of finding stable housing, inadequate access to drug and alcohol treatment, and lack of job training.
4. Between sixty and seventy percent of former inmates find themselves jobless up to one year after being released.
5. The issues of housing, treatment, and employment are critical. They are also tangible. But there's another significant issue facing former inmates that is difficult to track: the difficulty of navigating a world that you've been secluded from for years, or even decades.

LEAVING CAPTIVITY WHEN YOU ARE ON THE SEX REGISTER

Anyone who commits a crime involving a sexual nature has two parts of his criminal sentence. There is the standard sentence: prison time or probation. Then there is another sentence that begins as soon as the first ends: the sex offender registry. In most states, his name, picture, residential and job information will be listed on the world wide web for all to see, permanently.

This type of sentence may seem appropriate for some sexual predators, who is the reason it was designed to begin with in the nineteen nineties. The purpose was supposed to be not punishment but prevention. The theory was that sexual predators were unable to control their urges, and the government could not do enough to keep them away from children, so the job of avoiding sexual predators needed to fall to the parents. So by giving parents information about where the predators were, bad things could be avoided.

But nearly thirty years later, the sex offender register hasn't worked as a preventive tool. Instead, it has caught thousands of people in a tightly woven net of legal sanctions and social stigma. Registered sex offenders are constrained by where, with whom, and how they can live—then further constrained by harassment or shamming from neighbors and prejudice from employers.

Some people on the sex offender registry have had their lives ruined for relatively minor or harmless offenses. For example, a statutory rape in which the victim is a high school grade younger than the offender. Or someone urinating in a public park. Both examples may need some repercussions, but do they warrant devastation for the rest of the offender's life?

This happens often in the criminal justice system: something designed for one purpose ends up getting used for something else. It happened because people can't agree on what society wants to do with criminals to begin with. Do we punish or rehabilitate?

Sex offender registries were designed to protect children from pathological sexual predators. Like a lot of other "seemed like a good idea at the time" tough on crime laws, the sex offender regime was built under legislation during President Bill Clinton's term. Now, regardless of what kind of sex offense is committed, though, all the perpetrators end up on the same list.

Preventing someone from reoffending depends on what he's done and who he is. A one-size-fits-all registry makes that impossible. Laws can make it impossible for sex offenders to find housing or get a job, for years after they have completed their sentences.

In California, there are over 230 mandatory restrictions on sex offenders. Offenders cannot live with an adopted child, cannot work in public parks, cannot enter school grounds, cannot live in facilities for the chronic ill, cannot drive tow trucks, and cannot sell hearing aids. Many offenders are harassed in person, and even more via social media, mail and phone calls. Sometimes, even the families are harassed.

Most people are not sentenced to prison for life; their punishments are only supposed to last a certain amount of time. Having your life constrained and restricted even after your sentence is over might be a fact of life in our current criminal justice system, but that's not the way punishment is supposed to work.

TWEET:
If you stop actively looking for the good in people you will only find the flawed, evil characteristics that make us human. But the God in us will be revealed—and we can find it by simply looking harder. In my prison world, I must be on an active hunt.

THE TIME WAS 10:55 A.M., AUGUST 29TH, 2020

My time was finally up and a mixed bag of emotions filled my heart and soul. Excited about leaving my cage but also overwhelmed with grief from leaving dear friends whom I've been through various battles with. I walked out of *Cell 203* with Tony by my side for the last time with my guitar on my back and all my other memories, books and the information I've accumulated over the years I called "My how to survive in freeworld manual."

While walking down the stairs from my cell to the unit exit door, I couldn't help but notice the eyes on me. The other one hundred twenty-seven guys that were not leaving prison today all watching me take my final walk through the unit. I took a moment and grieved for them, realizing what they must be feeling at this moment, surely wishing it was them leaving captivity today. To break the silent tension in the space, I started singing "Na Na Na Na, Na Na Na Na, Hey Hey Hey Goodbye." Everyone joined in as we walked out of the pod. Tony and I walked through the yard getting high fives, dabs, God blesses and love ya bros. We walked to the gate together knowing this would be the last time on this side of heaven we would see each other.

We reached the point where I would have to go and he stay, so we embraced again. He gave encouragement as he always did and I attempted to give encouragement as well. I watched Tony walk back up the hill to the cage we called home for so many years, the one where we laughed, cried, ate, and shared memories as comrades do who endure horrific times together.

I sat in yet another small cage before my release waiting for personnel to bring paperwork for me to sign. I'm still not sure what I signed because all I cared about was moving a few feet to the other side of the fence where my friends Chris and Cindy were there to welcome me back to freedom. Until that point, I feared something would go wrong, like they usually do in prison, and they would find a problem with my release and I would be walking back up that hill to *Cell 203*.

Eventually, a prison staff person came in, exasperated with, "I don't have time for this today. I'm not twenty people, I can only do so much." I couldn't help but think, "That may be true, but you will be going home in a few hours, so just get me out of this cage." But like a good inmate, I kept all those feelings bottled up as trained to do by years of dehumanization and disrespect by staff. The guard placed a GPS monitor on my ankle helping me to remember that I'm still property of the Department of Corrections. The guard tagging an animal before being released back into his natural habitat.

While walking down the hill, where freedom was just feet away, I glanced back to the guard shack and noticed and marked the time was 10:55 a.m. I saw just up ahead, Chris and Cindy, ready to receive this broken vessel. When I embraced Chris, it had special meaning. He had been there for the last hug before I entered prison, ten years earlier. What a full circle moment, praise God.

Yet another officer greeted me outside the prison gates in order to ensure my GPS was working properly. She drove behind my escape vehicle, and pulled us over several times to check why my GPS leash wasn't working, until it was finally fixed and she drifted off out of site.

After years only standing on land, the motion of the car left me sick to my stomach. So we pulled over to have my first meal at Arby's at a filling station. I couldn't eat because I was busy throwing up. The only way to tame my motion sickness was for me to drive. Chris looked a little scared, it had been a while since I drove. He actually lost his color a bit. I started feeling much better so I called my mother while driving eighty miles an hour down the highway. Chris kept his eyes closed during most of this time, probably praying we would be safe.

The sights were amazing as if I had a new lease on life: trees, rivers, lakes, people not in uniforms and something about the air smelled cleaner, fresher. I swear I could smell freedom; my senses were awakened. When we arrived at our hotel several things started to send me into a panic attack. So many moving parts around me, people walking in front of me, in back of me, people talking on their phones, elevators, different colors and choices to make. I felt like everyone was staring at me like I was some kind of freak. This was most definitely sensory overload for me. For years I had to constantly watch the people around me in fear I would accidently walk into a gang fight, get shanked, or robbed. Inmates will typically find a wall to stand in front of in order to decrease the approach points to him. New sounds I wasn't used to, caused the hair on my arms to stand up and my stomach to quiver.

Hours later we went to a nicer restaurant for dinner where we met my brother Scott and wife Sara. It was a beautiful reunion after so many years away from my brother. For so long I was mad at him for not writing but the minute I saw him all was forgiven. The food server set my plate in front of me with a huge steak and potato. Beside the plate were metal utensils, a fork, a spoon, a knife. The feel of metal on my fingers felt strange, as if I was having to learn how to eat all over again. For years all I had to eat with was a plastic spork. All of these utensils sitting around me would have been shank material in prison, now I'm sitting casually at a table full of killing equipment. The first bite of steak was also greeted with the taste of metal from the fork. Strange, very strange.

The roller coaster of a day was coming to a close. I looked around the table at the faces of so many people I longed to be reunited with and felt so grateful and humble. But the faces of the ones I left behind were also front and center. I couldn't help but notice that the clock indicated that almost twelve hours had elapsed since I walked out of prison. It had been a full circle moment of emotions. I knew that my life must involve helping my brothers still in captivity find freedom or help them better the conditions of their confinement.

> **TWEET:**
> Social separation may be necessary at times. However, such separation should seek to create the space for transformative justice to assess the needs of survivors, those who have caused harm and the community—ultimately resulting in the restoration of the individual to his community.

DEATH WAITS FOR NO ONE

My father endured the ten years of my incarceration and was now ill and on his death bed. During the years I had spent in prison, I was constantly praying that my parents, both in their eighties, would survive my incarceration so I could see them once again. My parents had long been divorced and lived in two different states, my mom in Texas and my dad in Florida. Both a long way from Tennessee where I had to live after I was released from the Tennessee Department of Corrections.

Certainly I would have chosen to live with either of my parents upon release if I could have gotten permission from the Community Supervision office to do so. My immediate supervising officer wanted me to be able to go, but was tied down by the system that she had bought into, hook, line and sinker. Since I was required to be a registered sex offender, the rest of my days on earth, would be monitored, tracked, explored, and would never be actually free to my own will. Many friends in the Tennessee area offered me places to live, but these were all rejected as well due to their closeness to schools, churches, daycares, parks, decisions by homeowner's associations, and who knows what else.

All of that didn't matter much to my father or me during his time of need. Certainly, if I talked to the right person in charge, a moral and ethical decision would be made that would allow me to go to my dying father's bedside. Certainly, all the years I had spent in prison doing my time, staying out of trouble, bettering myself, would be recognized at this moment.

Hours passed, days passed, without permission. Finally, it was too late, my father died and that was that.

> **TWEET:**
> Spend time with people you will be thinking
> about on your deathbed.

RESILIENCE

Often people will say that when you leave prison you should try to forget it, walk away, and don't look back. Of course, that is easier said than done, in fact, I'm not sure why anyone would not want to forget the horrors that they have endured and lived through while in prison, but that's simply not possible. Resilience is the ability to adapt to difficult situations and still be able to thrive. People walking out the door of prison into the freeworld are resilient, remarkable beings that have lasted the dehumanizing drama of life behind bars and managed to walk out alive. A testimony to the human spirit.

Many times throughout the day on this side of the fence, I have to remind myself that I am capable, I'm worthy, I'm resilient. The system that drives the forces of incarceration are set up to constantly remind you that you are none of those things. I had to establish realistic goals for my freedom under the restrictions that the State held over me. Thinking too much about what I couldn't do was preventing me from doing the things I could do.

Fresh out of the joint the first thing I longed to do was to see my mother and hold her in my arms. It wasn't as easy as hopping in the car and taking off to Texas, where she lives. I had to request permission from the Supervision Office to travel, giving a location, the amount of time I would be gone, and who I would be staying with. This took time for them to approve my request. Delayed gratification has become my new normal.

I had just left prison where it was normal to have staff talk to you like a slave or a piece of property with no value. I was surprised to encounter that same type of communication with the State Offices that deal with people on the sex register. I had done my time for my crimes and understood that I was obligated to report and maintain the various restrictions they had placed on me. Every time I reported to the office, I was told to sit down and wait. It was not uncommon to have to wait for hours and then be told they would not be seeing me and to come back another day. When I was seen, the Officer was rude and disrespectful and could never answer any question that I had about my supervision. I can see how it would become very difficult to find a job that would be so understanding of having to leave work and stay gone for hours and then have to do it all over again because you couldn't be seen at the scheduled time.

So yes, I'm resilient. I took all that garbage and still enjoyed the visit with my mother who had waited ten long years to have her son in her house. As welcoming as my mother was into her home it was not a place that I could live. Her residence was not approved by the State as an acceptable place for me to live. I could not live with my own mother because of the location of her property. Finding a home would become my next challenge.

TWEET:

What is the worst thing you have ever done? Write it on a sticker and put the sticker on the front of your shirt, and wear it everywhere you go. Nothing you can ever do will cover that label up—everything is seen through that stain. This is a convict's life—*forever*.

FINDING A PLACE TO CALL HOME

Upon release from prison, I was anxious to find a place I could call home, a place to feel safe and a place that I had the key to get in and could always get out. My search and battle started long before my release. I submitted home plan after home plan to the prison reentry coordinator whose job it was to help inmates secure housing and to get a driver's license and social security card. One after another, the housing I found was denied by the Supervision Office that is over those on the sex register. My father's house was unacceptable, too close to a school. My mother's house unacceptable, along with a host of other friends who offered me housing, unacceptable as well. Before leaving prison the only approved housing I could secure was an old run down motel that had been converted into one room apartments. In order to secure it and have a place to live after release, I had to pay the place over a thousand dollars to make sure the apartment would be available. That amount of money took me over two years of prison work and scrimping by to save. It was in a shady part of town and the room was not much improved from the prison cell I had just left. But it would allow me to leave prison with a place to rest my head.

Living at the roach motel was incentive to get moving on finding a more permanent dwelling space. A few organizations that try and help ex-offenders find acceptable housing, gave me lists of possible landlords in the area where I was trying to live, but those lists did not turn out any legitimate potential homes. Being on the registry severely limits your housing possibilities. Over seventy-five percent of my county was eliminated by an exclusion zone. These zones state that I cannot live or work within one-thousand feet of a park, school, and most churches. So once you are out of prison, a person on the registry has two battles right off—being labeled an ex-felon and then the real Scarlet Letter of being on the sex register.

I recall vividly the emotions on the faces or in their voices when I would have to tell potential landlords about my past. One time, while in the apartment complex from the list given to me by Project Return, a landlord said she didn't think it would be a problem that I was an ex-felon. At this point I still had not told her that I was also on the register. Before I could, she dropped the ultimate bombshell, "Depends on what type of charge you have." I got the same feeling I had while in prison when I walked into a new pod and other inmates asked for my charge so they could decide whether to assault or extort money from me. The prison system has a class system all to itself. Murderers get the most respect, since bucking them seems ridiculous. But at the very bottom of the totem pole is sex offenders. Anyone labeled as such is subject to getting brutalized at will, or robbed and extorted. Flashbacks of my time on the inside flew through my brain as this landlord was judging me with that same prison mentality that I thought I had finally escaped.

The process of finding a home was a mental exercise of resilience, but a battle that I knew I had to win. I simply could not wrap my head around how the facts of my life were not playing out to the reality of my current existence. I had saved money to secure the things I needed, I had great credit, I had an excellent rental history from years ago, I had great references, and yet all of this was overshadowed by the fact that I was on the sex register.

Well over a year of exhaustive searching for a home, my day finally arrived. I met a landlord that said he would be happy to rent to me, the he didn't care about my past and was willing to give me a chance. My joy was overwhelming and that sense of fear that had built up in my soul was finally released. I moved into a lovely two-bedroom home and I was able to rest my head on my pillow, on my bed, in my bedroom, at my house. Praise God! My friends showered me with gifts for my new place and it quickly began to feel like home, welcoming me with love at the door each time I arrived.

I have a front porch where I placed two chairs and a little table. I will often sit out there and watch the sun go down, imagining that Tony is sitting there with me and we are talking about how crazy our lives had been in prison, and recounting how happy we are to be free.

> **TWEET:**
> I dream of a house that has a door that will not
> lock me in and not lock me out.
> A front porch, to sit and dwell on the day's
> events, and remember how good life is now
> that I'm free.

TWEET:
We all have a past, but someone who has been
incarcerated must start every conversation with
the circumstances that brought him to prison,
and then try to explain that he is now worthy of
love and acceptance.

NO HARM INTENDED—BUT SOME TAKEN

I was as nervous as a cat in a room full of rocking chairs when I met a friend for my first date since being released from captivity. She certainly checked a lot of the so-called boxes I had thought were necessary for a possible mate: appropriate age, no kids, Christian, played and loved music. We ordered our food and the conversation began:

Her
"Oh great to see you, you look great, please tell me more about yourself."

Me
"Blah blah blah blah blah"

Her
"Wow, new home, new job, new vehicle. It's amazing what God is doing in your life since you were released from prison. So tell me, how does someone like you end up in prison."

Me
"Blah blah blah blah blah"

Then the real interrogation began:

Her

How long were you married?
How old are your kids?
Do you still talk to them?
Who was your victim?
How did you do that?
What caused you to do that?
Did you get treatment for it while locked up or how about now?

I felt like my Miranda rights needed to be read to me and my attorney called. Certainly I understood that before any real and meaningful relationship could ever be formed with anyone, open and honest communication would be necessary about both of our pasts. But this seemed like a lot for the first date conversation. Trying to explain the complicated and bizarre circumstances that led to my incarceration takes more than a dinner to explore.

I admit, I was not prepared for this experience and wonder if I'll ever have the courage again to enter the world of dating.

TWEET:
I love to be loved, but you can't please
everybody. You could be a juicy ripe peach
and there'll still be someone who doesn't like
peaches.

SHAKEDOWN

One of the most humiliating and dehumanizing events that occur while you are incarcerated is the constant searching of your property done by prison staff. Any person who works at the prison, from a guard to the education secretary, has the right to enter your cell and go through all of your belongings, even reading your mail. This was done countless times during my prison sentence and it never got easier or less devastating. Even when you know that you don't have anything like drugs or shanks in your cell, you begin to worry about what they could possibly find that would result in sanctions or even segregation time.

I thought all of that sort of treatment was behind me once I had completed my ten years of captivity and was released into the freeworld, but I was greatly mistaken. While sitting on my front porch enjoying my day off, I received a phone call from the officers who supervisor people on the sex register. They told me to stay at home they were on their way to conduct a routine search. Four officers soon pulled up and began searching everything inside my house and even my vehicle parked in the driveway. One officer stayed with me and I couldn't help but release some of my exasperation onto to her over the ordeal.

I noticed the neighbors, all curious at the state vehicle parked out front and with uniformed officers examining my property, were all wide-eyed and I'm sure wondering what sort of vile character had moved into their lovely neighborhood. I wondered if they started complaining to my landlord if he would have second thoughts on renting me this property and kick me out. I wondered if the officers searching my home were corrupt because I had seen so many inside the prison do unscrupulous things when searching a cell.

All those helpless memories where my belongings were being rumbled through and disrespected from prison came to the surface and at that moment I was that same slave of the state who had no rights or say so over my own person. After they finally left and I was alone, it seemed like my house had just been burglarized. All the hard work of finding my home, my safe place to dwell, had been violated. How could I ever feel safe?

I knew that I had to get my mind wrapped around this whole idea that all of the trauma and craziness of prison was behind me. My new normal, even in the freeworld, was going to encompass a lot of the dehumanizing and degrading aspects that had been part of my ten years of incarceration. I had to find a way to deal with that truth both mentally and physically—because I could certainly see myself cussing out one of those officers tearing through my personal property and getting violated even further. God and a stiff drink was going to be needed.

There had to be some sort of advocacy for change in my future. I had to find ways to begin the uncomfortable discussion about what the people on the sex register deal with each day. And perhaps I could find a way to form a support group of people in my situation to discuss ways to improve our conditions and help each other out through the maze the state has created for us. I couldn't simply be satisfied with how it is, change has to happen, and I guess I must get moving on it.

> ### TWEET:
> We can't wait for someone else to make things better for us—we have to do what we can, where we are, with what we have. I have a voice, some thoughts, a loud voice and lots of email addresses.

STORIES FROM THE GROUP

While sitting in my roach infested room at Casablanca, the only place I could arrange to live after being released, I listened to the noises around me and it was traumatic—people yelling from nearby apartments, traffic on the street, honking horns, gun shots and a constant hum from electrical lights and faulty air-conditioning units. The smell of mold and mildew and recent bug chemicals sprayed around the rooms overwhelmed my senses. I realized that many people just like me were sitting in apartments like this who could not get approved for any better type of living because they were on the sex register. And like me, many were probably unaware of how to change the circumstances or if it was even possible to do so.

I began making calls to people I respected who worked on prison reform and other issues related to disenfranchised groups of people. Jeannie Alexander, founder of No Exceptions Prison Collective along with an attorney, Ryan Davis, offered the facts about what I was facing and the types of changes needed for the community of people on the sex register. This information began the idea of forming a support group of ex-offenders who were facing the same hurdles as I was. Ryan Davis agreed to be involved and helped answer legal questions and keep us on track as far as the law was concerned in our movements and decisions.

A group formed and the problems and life circumstances resulting from being on the sex register mounted up to a hill that seemed insurmountable. Here are a few of the stories from people in the support group:

Bobby:

I was so excited to get out of prison after being in for fifteen years. I've lived at Casablanca now for ten years. I can't keep a steady job cause of the negativity of being on the register. I can't save any money to find a better place, and who knows if I could find a better place that would take someone like me? I don't have any family and it's hard to find real friends out here that want to mess with anyone that lives in this part of town. I'm ashamed to tell anyone where I live because they would probably think I'm just some type of drug dealer living out of a trap house. Any don't even get me started on getting involved in a relationship. That seems so foreign of an idea that I don't even entertain it. I wonder why I even left prison, I had more freedom in there.

Carl:

None of this sex register crap was even talked about when I pled guilty to my crime years ago. While doing fifteen years in the joint, the state thought all of this shit up and makes it almost impossible to survive. The restrictions on living and working close to schools or churches make it almost impossible to find any real job. I've been home-less for almost two years and the state only cares that I come to the sex register office and let them know where I'm homeless at. Isn't that stupid. Most homeless shelters won't even allow you in if you are on the register. The state should have just put me down like a rapid dog if this is the life they had in mind for me.

Fred:

What I don't understand is that the state had me locked up for nearly twelve years and during that time never made any attempt to give me any programing, counsel-ing, or rehabilitative classes for the crimes that sent me to prison. And once I was out, all the state cared about was me paying them a weekly fee for GPS monitoring and classes where I'd go and sit until the hour was up, pay a fee and then leave. If I can't find a job how am I supposed to pay them a fee? I tried to kill myself once but it didn't work out. Now I'm just angry and live just to spite the state. I reached out to a church hoping for some spiritual guidance. When they found out I was on the register, they said they were not equipped to have someone like me attending their church. What in the hell does that mean?

Greg:

I have the shits all the time from my nerves. While I'm working or even at my apartment, I'm waiting on the police to come by and tear up my place. The police won't leave me alone. I've not violated one rule since being out, but I'm always worried they will find something to put me back in the joint. I barely survived the joint, so I can't go back. Sometimes I just want to catch a bus to somewhere and just keep traveling to the next somewhere. But that would mean a life on the run and always looking over my shoulder. Being on the register means you wear a sign on your back that says, "Come fuck with me."

There are plenty other stories from people who are dealing with life on the sex register. I pray the support group will be able to work through some of these issues and provide some hope and encouragement. I still find it difficult to accept compliments or praise from anyone. The years of dehumanizing treatment from prison and now from the community supervision people, have left me with a sense of shame and unworthiness that is hard to overcome. When Rev. Alexander told me she was proud of me for beginning the support group, I found myself uncontrollably crying off the side of the road. Developing your self-esteem after years of being told that you are worthless, and not wanted in the community, is a task that requires a deep faith in God and a willingness to forgive yourself. If we cannot forgive ourselves for our past transgressions, how in the hell can we expect anyone else too?

> **TWEET:**
> Sometimes you are forced to be a leader, not because you are the most intelligent, or even the most qualified—but because you are willing to pick up the sword and start swinging.

TWEET:
Some mornings I just want to stay in the
bed—the day holds too many obstacles. I place
one foot down, then the other, and begin my
moments. I can deal with moments.

IN CLOSING

I'm not sure how to close this in a hopeful manner to the people who have been incarcerated and respectful to the victims that brought me to this place in my life. In both instances it is important to understand that you should not be totally defined by your worst mistake. You cannot sit in a pit of despair the rest of your life because of the sins that put you there. If you do, you are not being respectful to yourself or the victims you have left behind. That state puts you in a phase of not being able to function at all. And you need to be able to improve yourself, reflect on the things that brought you to prison, and make efforts to do better. It will be difficult to navigate the system that is set up for you to fail, but eventually you will map out your landscape and the travel will seem less and less bumpy.

One of the most important things to a successful transition back into society is to build a network of supportive people. You may find these people at churches, your work place, organizations, or other means you find to gather with folks. I started this process of building community a long time before I left prison and it has paid off for me. Pay attention to the people God puts in your life, they are there for a reason. Many times you may not even understand why at the time. If possible, stay in contact with them through calls or mail—that begins your networking for your future.

Your own resilience will be tested, it's up to you to be kind and gentle to yourself. The picture you drew of your future life while you were locked up will be different when faced with the reality of freedom. This picture was difficult for me to accept at first. It took numerous failed attempts. But through those trials I was able to invent a new set of lenses to view this picture of my life. So in those moments of despair remember to hold on to whatever your faith is and lean on the current community of support you have built, then pick yourself up slowly, wipe off your glasses and see that you are free from count times and lockdowns.

My heart still aches for my brothers I left behind the razor wire. And now the new peer group that I have formed of people going through the same struggles as I am, is motivating me to bring awareness to the illogical system of rules and regulations placed on people leaving incarceration, especially those who remain on a sex register. Part of me wants to slip into oblivion and blend in and disappear in order to just exist with as little difficulty as possible. It's time, however, that those of us you have left the system of injustice scream about the craziness until someone lends an ear. I don't know where this will take me, but I have my loud speaker in hand and intend to shout until I can't anymore. I pray the man I am today will honor my victim and will honor God. Dear brothers inside the cage and those who have been released, please hang on, just hang on!

> **TWEET:**
> Some things must be told, be repeated, be shouted—until someone hears your cry. In silence lives the atrocities that we perpetrate towards each other. Get on the soap box and preach!

RESOURCE GUIDE

It can be overwhelming to have someone you love incarcerated. The unknowns and unpredictability's of confinement are scary and full of governmental bureaucracies. Remember, you are a taxpayer who pays the salaries of government officials, including prison administration and officers. Your loved one may be locked up and void of most rights, but you are not. So use these tips to overcome your fear and get moving towards knowledge. I use the pronoun "he, him" to refer to an inmate below. Obviously there are many females incarcerated and I mean no disrespect to them. I'm simply reflecting on my experience since I'm at a male prison. This guide could be applied to a women's prison as well.

a. Know the telephone numbers, addresses, and names of the prison officials, including the Warden, Assistant Wardens, Chief of Security, and Medical Administrator. Keep their telephone numbers and email addresses handy. Most all of this information can be found on-line or by simply calling the prison and asking.

b. Do not be intimidated by the dismissing rhetoric prison administration may use to put you off. They may say things like:

   1. That information is not available.
   2. Who are you, why are you calling?
   3. This is prison, it's going to be hard.
   4. He has to toughen up.
   5. Don't believe all the lies these convicts tell you.
   6. He is safe, being fed, and has all the care he needs.

c. When you do call, have your loved one's prison number available. Don't make frivolous calls complaining about things like your son did not get his Ramen noodles in his commissary package, or he doesn't like his current cell mate. Types of legitimate times to call or email would be:

1. You have not heard from your loved one in an unusual amount of time.
2. You feel that he may be in a depressed state where harm may be done.
3. He is not receiving adequate medical care for a condition.
4. He is not receiving his medication for a chronic illness.
5. He is being bullied or pressured into doing things out of his character.

It is easy for an inmate to get lost in the system when no one on the street is advocating for him.

> **TWEET:**
> I get lots of letters from parents of newly incarcerated folks worrying about how to best help their child. Effective advice is encouraging the child to find community, build friendships, and tap into their gifts and talents. Life, and a good life, is still before them.

Encourage Those Incarcerated to do Positive Things

Like it or not your loved one is incarcerated. While in confinement, he can use this time to improve himself, his skills, and his education. Unless he is in segregation, he will most likely be allowed books and educational material. Reading material is the lifeblood of us incarcerated. We can always turn to a book to take our minds away from this razor wire to places far away. I've started book clubs to encourage people to read and form community, and now we often get the authors of the books we are reading to come and visit the prison to discuss their book. You will be amazed at how many authors are excited to visit a prison. This experience is transformative and can change the lives of the author and the inmates. When communicating with your loved one, here are some suggestions on how to encourage him to stay positive and involved in community. Building community in prison is what keeps you safe and emotionally stable.

1. Inquire what he is doing, what he is reading, what he is watching on television. Find a common book or program that you can virtually watch together or discuss when you talk.

2. Inquire what activities he is participating in: card games, religious programs, education classes, etc.

3. If he is interested in correspondence classes, find out what is allowed at his prison. If he does not know, you can call the school principal or the facility staff at the prison to ask what types of material he can receive. Receiving regular material

to work on in the cell is a great way to learn and to keep your mind occupied from the chaos around you.

4. Some prisons allow arts and craft material. If so, this can be a great way to stay busy and constructive. During my time I've made homemade cards, learned to knit and crochet, cross stitched, embroidered, and painted, among many other activities. I've seen inmates become masters at various crafts to the point where they have been able to sell their work for income.

5. As an outside supporter, you can be instrumental in being the push to encourage him to stay involved. Being a lone sheep among the wolves is not a smart strategy. This doesn't mean joining a gang—but making friends and communing with people that share similar interests. When predators observe inmates who are always alone, they mark them as prey. But if they see that an inmate has a group of friends around, the predators are less likely to risk attack or bullying.

6. Find out what the mail policy is at the prison. What type of photos are allowed, and if clips of newspapers and magazines are allowed? Sending photos, even if printed on a home computer printer, and clips of interesting articles from newspapers and magazines, are great ways to keep a dialogue between you and your loved one. Keeping their mind engaged in the world and community allows them to see past the existence of prison—even if for a short time. I have several pen pals who clip out articles they know I would find interesting. I love cooking and watching cooking shows, so I often get clips of recipes or articles about restaurants in the mail. Another friend always sends me funny cartoons he finds in the newspaper or in magazines about once a week. He says when he sees something funny he tears it out and puts it in an envelope he has on his desk, and then mails it out each Monday. I always look forward to reading the things people have taken the time to clip out for my enjoyment. My aunt would send me her church bulletin each week with a little note. I felt like I was a part of her world in that moment.

7. Getting mail in prison is like receiving a tiny gift from the outside world. Even if it is just a card or a few sentences on

a piece of paper, receiving regular mail helps the inmate feel connected to those he loves. Encourage your family members and friends to be pen pals with the inmate. If possible, use colorful paper and ink. Color is bland in prison, so anything that has a bright color is appreciated.

Dealing with Prison Policies And Structures

All prisons have a set of rules and policies that they are required to maintain and follow. Of course, we all know how loose these rules can be maintained. It's a slippery slope. These policies are public record and you should be able to acquire a copy either on-line or by requesting a copy from the facility. There are two particular areas where policies and structures are extremely important—inmate packages and visitation practices.

1. Most prisons have very particular rules about what sort of packages an inmate can receive. You can probably find out the vendor allowed and the time period the inmate can order from on the prison website, or by calling and inquiring at the prison. Don't just order a package without talking with the inmate, because he may not be allowed to receive the package, or he may have already received his allotted packages for the quarter. Also, he may desperately need particular items that you are not aware of, and if you should order on your own, it could prevent him from being able to acquire the things he really needs.

2. Prisons will furnish the inmate with uniforms, boots, t-shirts, underwear, linens and bedding. If the inmate wants tennis shoes, recreation clothing like shorts or sweat pants, watches, and various other items, he must order a package or have someone order one for him. These items can get expensive, and more than likely the inmate will be asking you for help to purchase these items. This can get expensive. It's a good time to develop a support system of people who care about the inmate who would contribute to purchasing the needed items.

This will help alleviate some of the burden from you and allow others who would like to help have an opportunity to do so. Social media can be helpful in these endeavors. Consider establishing a group email or group in Twitter or Facebook, where a support system for you and your loved one incarcerated can be developed.

SHAME IS DAMAGING

It's hard to talk about someone you love being incarcerated, perhaps even shameful. My mother couldn't bring herself to talk to her friends about me being in prison for several years. She felt like they were judging her as well as the difficulty in having to talk about the crimes that brought me here, seemed too much for her. It shouldn't be your cross to bear, but it will be, unfortunately. I suggest you rip off the band-aid as quickly as possible. One of my friend's mother prepared a group email that said something like this:

> "John is in prison. It rips my heart out and I will always love him. The details are public record, so if you are interested you can go there. My job as his mom is to love him, pray for him, and help him cope in an environment that is scary and harsh. I hope that you will help me in this endeavor with prayer and encouragement. If you would like to write him, I encourage you to do so. His address is . . ."

An email worked for her, but you may find that a group meeting or group letter would work for you. But get it over with quickly. Spitting out the truth gets rid of the shame and replaces it with a stark reality of the situation. There is no time to be playing games at this point. My friend's mom said that the group email was the most liberating send that she ever had. And amazingly, she received overwhelming support from people she did not expect. Keeping skeletons in the closet only allows rumors, lies and misinformation to develop that is often worse than the truth.

Don't be ashamed to talk about good or bad things in your life to your loved one incarcerated. My dad used to say he would feel guilty telling me about happy moments or even sad ones he was experiencing because he didn't want to burden me. What he didn't know is that I longed to hear all those little details of what he and mom were experiencing. An inmate needs to experience all the good and bad along with you, just like he needs you to do with his good and bad moments. Life's moments don't stop happening when your loved one is incarcerated. In fact, life's moments become more intense where the entire support system needs to be involved.

There will be some people that will try and shame you for staying in communication with someone incarcerated. They may have heard or seen on the news the terrible things that were done that led a person to prison. And more than likely, they were terrible. So many times outsiders will be reluctant to tell their friends that they have a prison pen pal or friend that's incarcerated. When I am meeting someone new, like a pen pal, I start out with a frank conversation. It goes something like this:

> I am so grateful that you are interested in writing. I want you to know that I am guilty of the crime that brought me here, so if you are looking for a wrongfully convicted person, I'm not him. But I'm not the same man that committed the crime. Even though I deserve the prison sentence I received, I certainly pray and hope for mercy. If given the opportunity, I would love to get to know you and for you to get to know me, the real me, that has developed over decades of incarceration. I promise to be honest with you and will welcome any questions or concerns you have.

As an outsider writing to a person in prison, you should expect and require the inmate to be honest and open with any question you may have. But don't write just to feel good about throwing a dog a bone, write with an expectation of developing a real friendship. A bunch of feel good rhetoric is not what anybody needs or desires. As far as those that will ridicule you for having a friend in prison—they will understand quicker than you may expect. The number of people being incarcerated is growing and effecting more and more families. More than likely, every household has someone incarcerated or knows someone who is. They will certainly hope that their loved one has people who care for them when they are on the other side of the razor wire.

> **TWEET:**
> Even when we go to bed feeling defeated and overwhelmed, we must get up the next day with optimism and enthusiasm, that the new day will bring clearer understanding, a new resolve and a resounding hope. If we don't the pit of depression is waiting for us, and it's no place to be.

Build a community of support for yourself and the incarcerated person

Don't put yourself in a bubble and block out everyone, because you will need support in a variety of ways. Hopefully, you have family and friends already who will be there for you. But there are also many support groups for loved ones of the incarcerated that will understand the situations and emotions you are experiencing. You will find some of those groups in our resource section.

A few of my friends on the inside have loved ones that visit them regularly who discovered they live in close proximity to each other. So they developed a carpool to save on gas and to simply have company to and from the prison. During these drives, they have formed a friendship and have each other to talk to and discuss issues that many others would not understand. As important as it is for you to build a community of support, your inside loved one needs to do the same. Encourage him to participate in activities and programs that will build community. Just as you will need to grieve and rejoice over occasions in your life with people around you, he will need to do the same with a group of insiders.

When my parents died, if I had not had a group of friends that were there, it would have been difficult to process the grief and to function. You knowing that your inside loved one has a support group, and he knowing you have one as well, will be a comfort to each of you. I have found in my group that when a loved one dies, we plan a memorial. We get the community together, pray, allow our grieved friend to express stories about the person he lost, and experience together, the pain. Spreading it out in little doses to people wanting to carry a load is a relief to the spirit.

You also need community to enjoy and rejoice—birthdays, holidays, and other special occasions. We threw our friend Carl, a thirty-year wedding anniversary party. His wife celebrated on the street with her friends and Carl, inside with his friends. When they talked and visited later they were able to share the fun experiences they each had. It's a way to create memories and not get fixed on concentrating on not being together.

Many churches have prison ministries and are active in prison and jails in the community. Find out if your church has one and be a resource to them providing information about the needs of the incarcerated and the needs of loved ones.

Let people in your community know what you need. Now is not the time to be bashful or ashamed about your situation. More than likely, you will be dealing with your loved one incarcerated for years not days—and that's a long time not to have people in your corner. So what might you need help from your community?

1. I need a babysitter so I can go visit my loved one.
2. I need to vent over the frustration of dealing with crazy prison politics.
3. I'm feeling lonely; you want to have coffee?
4. I need prayer.
5. I'm having trouble making ends meet this month—I could use some help with food or funds.
6. My family could use professional therapy; do you know of a therapist that deals with families of incarceration?
7. I need: (Fill in the blank)

The point is, don't be afraid to ask, nothing is too miniscule or great to put it into the universe.

Narrow your focus of activism so you can laser in on needed and legitimate issues

If you want to change anything about the prison system you must get political. The prison only changes when politicians change policies and laws. So if you are serious about advocating for any legitimate change in the culture of US prisons, get to know your elected officials. Select the most important issues to you and stay laser focused on those. If you are on social media find people who share your passion and begin email campaigns, Twitter storms, Facebook accounts, and any other means to get your message to the public.

For instance, if your loved one who is incarcerated is dealing with medical issues that the prison will not resolve, try dealing with the prison administration first—then go up the chain of command from there. Don't be afraid to contact the media with your complaints, and keep a record of all the calls, letters, emails you send regarding the issue. I have seen a simple call from a newspaper to the prison inquiring about a person's medical situation, resolve the matter expediently. The last thing the prison wants is negative publicity of any kind. It's a money making business that they don't want interrupted.

Vague hyperbole about the prison system gets lost in the universe. Therefore, be precise about your complaints and desire for whatever change you are advocating. A campaign promoting "Prison Reform" sounds good and is true, but is way too vague to accomplish very much. You may consider making a list of your top three complaints, which may change occasionally. You can then focus in on these items until you wear out the ears of the elected officials who are in charge of creating and changing them.

> ### TWEET:
> Some outsiders and insiders say, "I wish I had time to advocate for prison reform, or to write letters to politicians." But the fact is if you really want to do something, you'll find a way. If you don't, you'll find an excuse.
> *Preach!*

RESOURCE GUIDE

Listed below are some of the organizations and groups that may be beneficial to the families and loved ones of those incarcerated:

Angel Tree
Telephone: 800–552–6435
Address: 44180 Riverside Parkway
Lansdowne, VA 20176
Email: angeltree@pfm.org
Website: http://www.prisonfellowship.org/about/angel-tree/
Provides Christmas gifts and the gospel message to children on behalf of their incarcerated parents in partnership with local churches. Programs throughout the year include summer camping and mentoring.

Big Brothers Big Sisters National Office
Address: 230 North 13th Street
Philadelphia, PA 19107
Phone: (215) 567–7000
Fax: (215) 567–0394
Email: actioncenter@bbbs.org
Website: https://www.bbbs.org
A one-to-one mentoring organization for children.

Children of Incarcerated Parents Mentoring
Telephone: 410–532–6864
Address: 403 Markland Ave.
Baltimore, MD 21212
Email: natloffice@ndmva.org
Website: https://www.ndmva.org
Notre Dame—AmeriCorps's CHIP program provides one-on-one mentoring for children affected by parental incarceration. Partners with area schools and social service agencies to provide educational support for youth and adults.

Family Services
Telephone: 305–864–5553
Address: 9540 Collins Avenue, P.O. Box 547127
Surfside, FL 33154
Email: receptionist@aleph-institute.org
Website: https://www.aleph-institute.org
Assist Jewish families and children of those currently incarcerated connecting them with local community support, assisting with travel expenses to visit the inmate and setting up support between the families of those incarcerated.

Girl Scouts Beyond Bars
Telephone:(800) GSUSA 4 U (800–478–7248) or (212) 852–8000
Address: 420 5th Avenue
New York, NY 10018
Email: misc@girlscouts.org
Website: http://www.girlscouts.org
The goals of the Girl Scouts Beyond Bars (GSBB) program are to lessen the impact of parental separation due to incarceration, to foster the personal and social development of girls and their mothers, and to provide girls with the opportunity to participate with their parents in the Girl Scout Leadership Experience. Parents and their daughters take an active leadership role in the planning and implementation of Girl Scout program activities and also participate in facilitated discussions about family life, conflict resolution, and the prevention of violence and drug abuse. After release, parents and

daughters can continue to participate in troop meetings in their communities, making Girl Scouting a consistent presence in their lives.

Hope House
Telephone: 301–408–1452
Address: PO Box 60682
Washington, DC 20039
Email: cfennelly@aol.com
Website: https://www.hopehousedc.org
Hope House has three main goals: to strengthen families and in particular, the relational bonds between children and their fathers imprisoned far from home; to reduce the isolation, stigma, shame and risk these families experience when fathers and husbands are imprisoned; and to raise public awareness about this most at-risk population.

KidsMates Inc.
Address: 21218 St Andrews Blvd, #720
Boca Raton FL 33433
Email: info@kidsmates.org
Website: www.kidsmates.org
KidsMates Inc. is a national non-profit organization co-founded by children of incarcerated parents. KidsMates Inc.'s advocacy raises awareness about the silent American epidemic of parental incarceration and its lifelong negative impacts to affected children. The organization implements initiatives aimed at improving outcomes, fostering resilience, and empowering children of incarcerated parents.

Institute on Violence, Abuse, And Trauma
Address: 10065 Old Grove Road, Suite 101
San Diego, CA 92131
Email: forensics@alliant.edu
Website: http://ivatcenters.org
Professional services offered at IVAT include conducting child custody evaluations, psychological testing, forensic evaluations, and conducting treatment of a variety of emotional and behavioral problems. Additional direct services available through IVAT

include individual, family, re-unification, and group therapy; supervised visitation; and parenting skills classes. Therapy is provided to people with a variety of different problems in our comprehensive program. All services are provided on a sliding fee scale.

The Messages Project
Address: PO Box 8325 9711
8th View St. Suite 11
Norfolk, VA 23503
E-mail: list@themessagesproject.org
Website: https://themessagesproject.org
Phone: No Phone
The Messages Project is focused on the children left behind when a parent is incarcerated in prisons in Virginia, Nebraska, and Missouri several times a year to create videotapes or DVDs from incarcerated parents to their children. The recordings are mailed home to children and families, often with a book that was read as part of the message.

National Parents and Families Network
Telephone: 717–943–2492
Address: P.O. Box 6745
Harrisburg, PA 17112
Website: https://www.nationalfamilysupportnetwork.org/standards
         -of-quality
Email: cstuartconsult@aol.com

1. Responsible Parenting Training and Consulting
2. Re-Entry, Recidivism Training and Consulting
3. Community Engagement Training and Consulting
4. Curriculum Writing and Consulting
5. Counseling and Consulting on Children of Incarcerated Parents
6. Lecturing and Workshops on issues of Incarceration as it pertains to the family unit and society as a whole
7. Consulting and Training on how to work with the prison and correctional system
8. Consulting and Training on Mentoring Children of Incarcerated Parents

No Exceptions Prison Collective
Telephone: 615-997-0698
Address: 701 Gallatin Road S. Suite 206
Madison, TN 37115
Website: https://www.noexceptionsprisoncollective.org
Email: theeda.noexceptions@gmail.com
No Exceptions Prison Collective is a grassroots initiative in Nashville, Tennessee, dedicated to ending carceral enslavement by advocating that no exceptions be made to the abolition of slavery. Founded and are led by individuals directly impacted by carceral slavery—both insiders (prisoners) and free world folk.

Parenting And Family Healing
Telephone: 570-523-0605
Address: 88 Bull Run Crossing, Suite 1
Lewisburg, PA 17837
Email: staff@bfsf.org
Website: https://www.bfsf.org
Provides parenting and family healing to incarcerated individuals; trains counselors, educators, and others in relational healing and peer governance models.

Prisoner Visitation and Support
Telephone: 215-241-7117
Address: 1501 Cherry Street
Philadelphia, PA 19102
Email: pvs@afsc.org
Website: https://www.prisonervisitation.org
PVS is the only nationwide, interfaith visitation program given access by the Federal Bureau of Prisons and the Department of Defense to visit all federal and military prisoners. They have 300 volunteers across the US who regularly visit at over 90 federal and military prisons.

Prison Mail
Telephone: 814–742–7500
Address: PO Box 1602
Altoona, PA 16603
Email: info@prisonmail.org
Website: https://www.prisonmail.org
Prison Mail simplifies communication and encourages constant correspondence between prisoners and their families and loved ones. It uses the convenience of the internet to allow those with incarcerated loved ones to send messages on a regular basis.

National CURE
Address: PO Box 2310
Washington, DC 20013
Email: cure@curenational.org
Website: https://www.curenational.org
Phone: 202–789–2126
International CURE organizes people incarcerated and their loved ones to bring about prison reform.

US Dream Academy
Telephone: 410–772–7143
Address: 10400 Little Patuxent Parkway, Suite 300
Columbia, MD 21044
Email: info@usdreamacademy.org
Website: https://www.usdreamacademy.org
Provides children in grades three through eight daily after-school programming that includes on-line academic enrichment, which is the cornerstone of the skill-building component, dream building, and character building. Homework assistance and one to one mentoring are also provided. Programs currently in Washington, DC; Baltimore, MD; East Orange, NJ; Philadelphia, PA; Orlando, FL; Houston, TX; Salt Lake City, UT; Memphis, TN; Los Angeles, CA; Indianapolis, IN.

Volunteers of America
Telephone: 703–341–5000
Address: 1660 Duke Street
Alexandria, VA 22314
Website: http://www.voa.org/Get-Help/National-Network-of
        -Services/Corrections
It provides literacy and family strengthening programming for incarcerated parents and their children. Parents take a class then read and record books. The recordings are given to the children along with a book bag, personal tape player and other supplies.

We Got Us Now
Telephone: 9173304222
Address: 63 Hamilton Terrace Suite 36,
New York, New York 10031
Email: ebony@wegotusnow.org
Website: https://www.wegotusnow.org
We Got Us Now is a national nonpartisan organization built by, led by and about children and young adults impacted by parental incarceration with the mission to *engage, educate, elevate* and *empower* our historically invisible population through the use of digital narratives, safe inclusive spaces and advocacy led campaigns to ensure our voices are at the forefront of strategic initiatives, practices and policies that will help to keep our families connected, create fair sentencing and end mass incarceration.

Wings Ministry and Wings for L.I.F.E.
Telephone: 505–291–6412
Address: 2270 D Wyoming Blvd NE #130
Albuquerque, NM 87112
Email: annedenfield@WingsMinistry.org
Website: https://www.WingsMinistry.org
Wings Ministry—Christ's unconditional love shared with all families of prisoners. Wings for L.I.F.E.—Life-skills Imparted to Families through Education.

> **TWEET:**
> When it's all over I don't want to wonder
> "If Only?"
> I want to breathe wherever I am, with full
> breaths of hope working to free the slaves.